FIRST DAILY

MILLION 30
ABERDEEN PRESS &
EVENING
Jayne Anderson

Press and Journal

THE FIRST 250 YEARS

1748 • 1998

Norman Harper

ABERDEEN JOURNALS

First published in Great Britain in 1997, and reprinted in 1998, by
ABERDEEN JOURNALS LTD
Lang Stracht, Mastrick, Aberdeen AB15 6DF

Written, designed and produced by Norman Harper

Cover design by Susan Bell
First Daily lettering by Melissa Dale

British Library Cataloguing-in-Publication Data. A catalogue record for this book is available from the British Library

Flexicover ISBN 0 9510642 9 0
Hardback ISBN 1 901300 00 5
Presentation edition ISBN 1 901300 01 3

This book is dedicated to the tens of thousands of staff of the Press and Journal and its component forebears each of whom helped to record 250 years of history and built a great newspaper in the process

Scanning and origination by
Icon Reprographics Ltd., Aberdeen

Printed via BPC-AUP Aberdeen Ltd.

Foreword
by HM Queen Elizabeth, the Queen Mother

CLARENCE HOUSE
S.W.1

To the Editor
PRESS AND JOURNAL

I was most interested to learn that in 1998 the Press and Journal is to celebrate its Two Hundred and Fiftieth Anniversary and I send my warmest congratulations on this achievement.

Since the first reports by James Chalmers after the Battle of Culloden, the Journal has circulated international and local news throughout Scotland, providing an important and valued service for people in all walks of life, both at home and abroad.

I offer to all those who work for the Press and Journal my best wishes for the future.

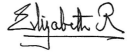

Elizabeth R

& JOURNAL
EVENING
EXPRESS

Press and Journal

THE FIRST 250 YEARS

1748 • 1998

Norman Harper

ABERDEEN JOURNALS

First published in Great Britain in 1997, and reprinted in 1998, by
ABERDEEN JOURNALS LTD
Lang Stracht, Mastrick, Aberdeen AB15 6DF

Written, designed and produced by Norman Harper

Cover design by Susan Bell
First Daily lettering by Melissa Dale

British Library Cataloguing-in-Publication Data. A catalogue record for this book is available from the British Library

Flexicover ISBN 0 9510642 9 0
Hardback ISBN 1 901300 00 5
Presentation edition ISBN 1 901300 01 3

This book is dedicated to the tens of thousands of staff of the Press and Journal and its component forebears each of whom helped to record 250 years of history and built a great newspaper in the process

Scanning and origination by
Icon Reprographics Ltd., Aberdeen

Printed via BPC-AUP Aberdeen Ltd.

Foreword
by HM Queen Elizabeth, the Queen Mother

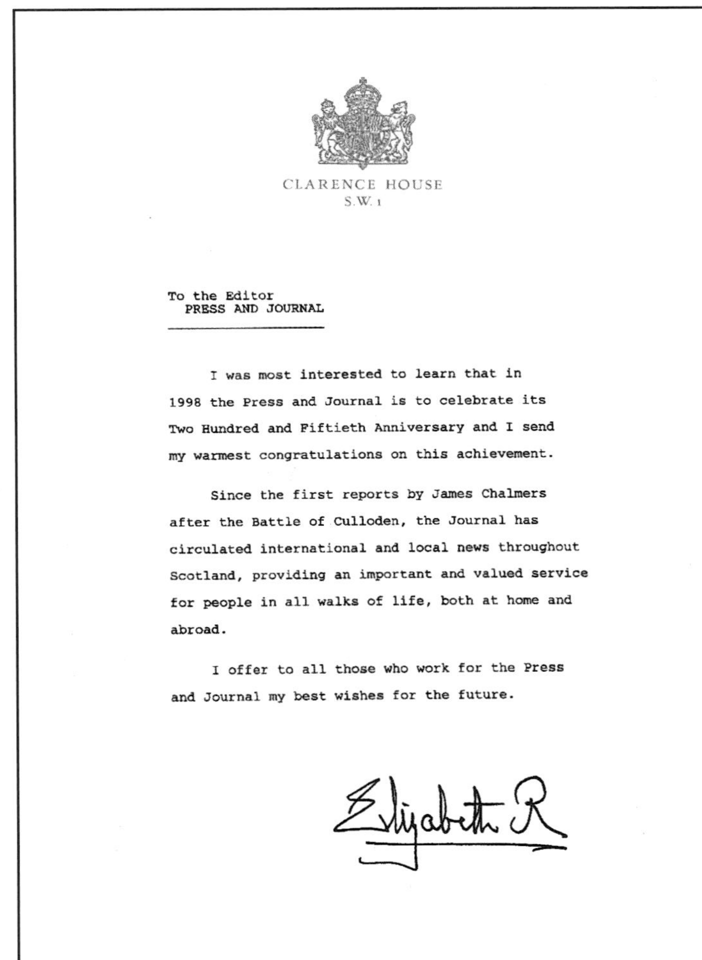

CLARENCE HOUSE
S.W.1

To the Editor
PRESS AND JOURNAL

I was most interested to learn that in 1998 the Press and Journal is to celebrate its Two Hundred and Fiftieth Anniversary and I send my warmest congratulations on this achievement.

Since the first reports by James Chalmers after the Battle of Culloden, the Journal has circulated international and local news throughout Scotland, providing an important and valued service for people in all walks of life, both at home and abroad.

I offer to all those who work for the Press and Journal my best wishes for the future.

Elizabeth R

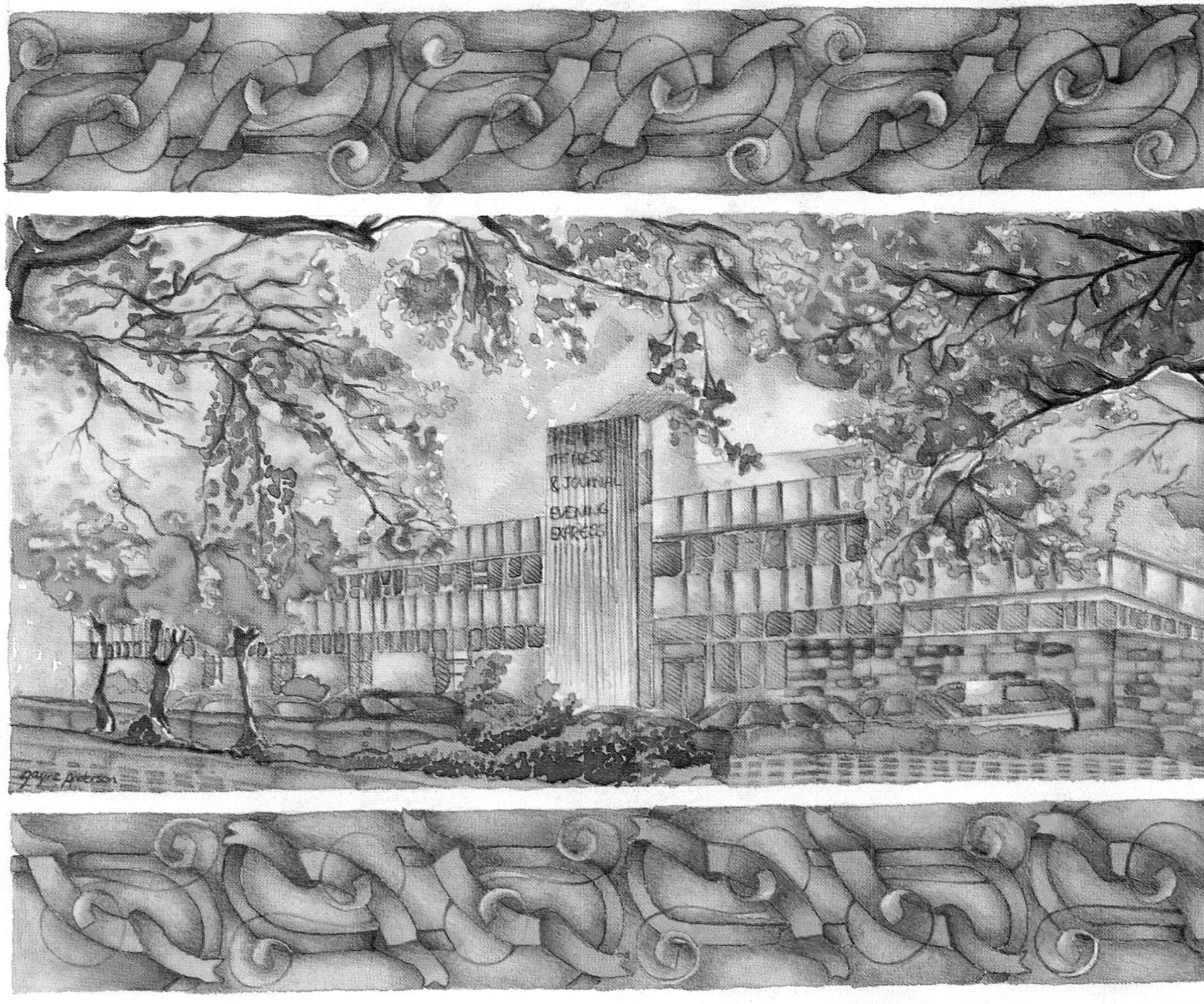
THE PRESS
& JOURNAL
EVENING
EXPRESS

Contents

Risky beginnings 8

Spice of competition 20

A difficult marriage 28

P&J goes to war 44

At death's door 56

Jimmy Grant's plan 76

Start spreading the news 98

New horizons 116

Teamwork 150

The next 250 170

Caught in the Act 178

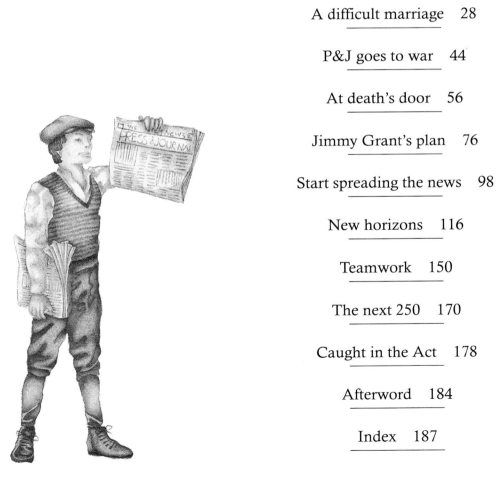

Afterword 184

Index 187

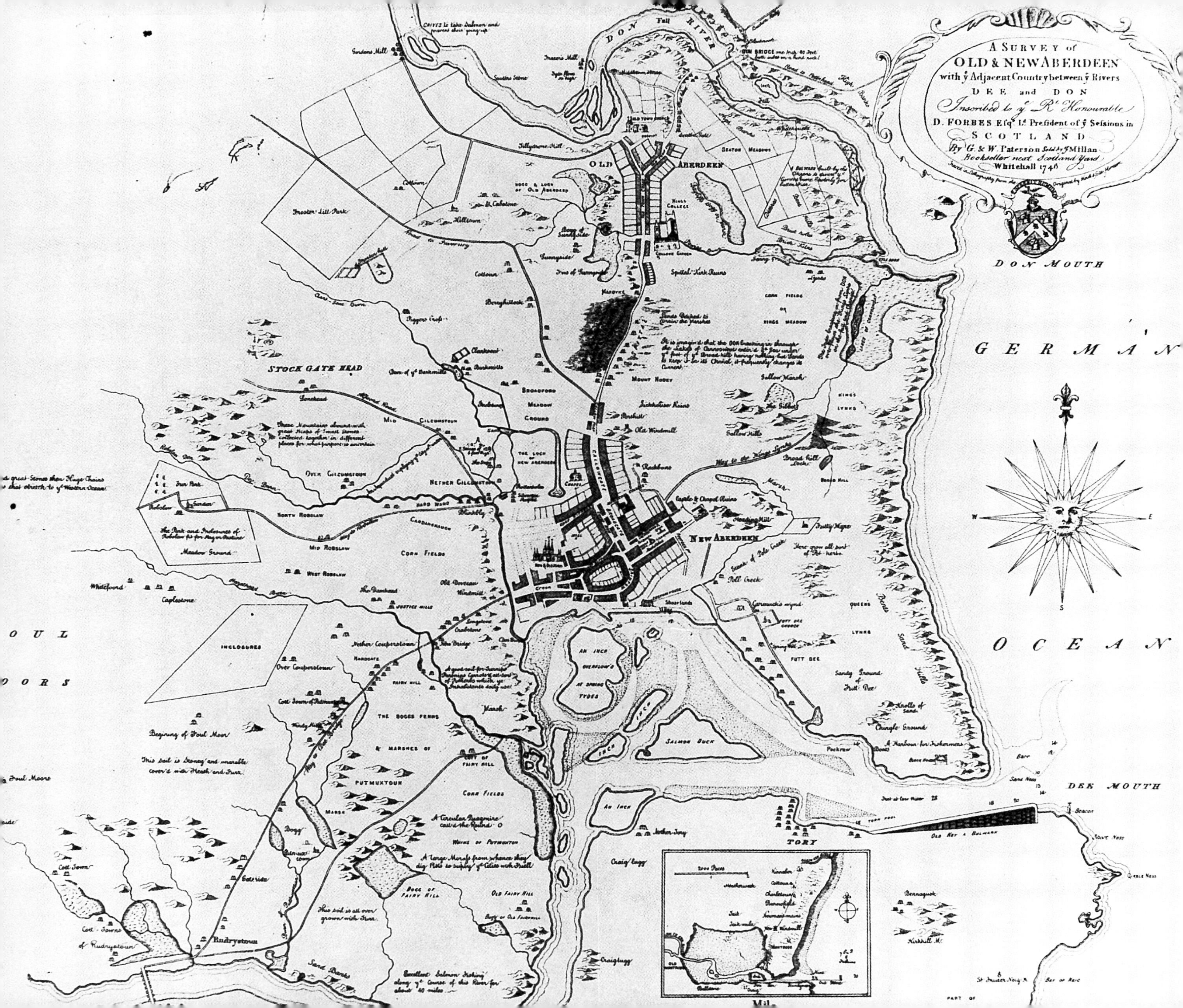
A SURVEY of
OLD & NEW ABERDEEN
with ye Adjacent Country between ye Rivers
DEE and DON
Inscribed to ye Rt Honourable
D. FORBES Esqr. Ld. President of ye Sessions in
SCOTLAND
By G. & W. Paterson Sold by J. Millan
Bookseller next Scotland Yard
Whitehall 1746
DON RIVER
DON MOUTH
OLD ABERDEEN
NEW ABERDEEN
GERMAN OCEAN
DEE MOUTH
STOCK GATE HEAD
Kings College
Seaton Meadows
Spittal Kirk Ruins
Corn Fields
Mount Hooly
Gallow Hills
Old Windmill
The Loch of New Aberdeen
Nether Gilcomstoun
Over Gilcomstoun
North Robslaw
Mid Robslaw
West Robslaw
Corn Fields
Inclosures
Foul Moors
Beginning of Foul Moor
The Boggs Ferns
Putmuxtoun
Futt Dee
Sandy Ground of Futt Dee
Salmon Duck
An Inch
Tory
Old Fairy Hill
Rudrystoun
Bog of Fairy Hill
Chingle Ground
A Harbour for Fishermen
Old Key & Bulwark
Girdle Ness

CHAPTER I

Risky business

ALL the best business beginnings come from a clash of frustration, inspiration and opportunity. This was the heady mix that gave birth to what is now the Press and Journal, Britain's biggest regional morning paper, its oldest daily and one of the three oldest English-language newspapers in the world.

The frustration, inspiration and opportunity were those of one man, a 34-year-old printer and son of the manse named James Chalmers. His was the vision and single-mindedness that created, then satisfied, the hunger for newspapers in Aberdeen. His was the work that ensured continued success where so many others were to fail later. He was the founding father of Britain's first media dynasty — a dynasty which lasted until 1929, when the Chalmers family grip on the North of Scotland newspaper scene ended with the death of company secretary D.M.A. Chalmers, great-great-grandson of the founder.

James Chalmers inaugurated a journal which has recorded the day-to-day events of city and country, nation and globe, for two and a half centuries. Throughout that time, it has stuck doggedly to the Chalmers founding tenet: that a sound and responsible newspaper tells its stories always in human terms, and in terms of their effect on its readers.

It has recorded and explained. It has cajoled and criticised. It has encouraged and supported. Like the area it has served, it has lived through changes unimaginable in the middle of the 18th century. It has recorded all of those changes, from the most momentous to the most humble, building a history of Scottish life unequalled anywhere.

All of this is rooted in the vision of one ambitious young man and his family.

The Chalmers story is one of unashamed populism and unabashed controversy; of surprisingly sophisticated attempts at manipulating this early market and of responding

A 1746 map of Aberdeen showing that the place was barely more than a large town when James Chalmers conceived the idea of a newspaper for the area.

James Chalmers (1713-1764) son of the manse, printer to the City of Aberdeen, ambitious businessman and founder of the Aberdeen's Journal, post-Culloden forerunner of the modern Press and Journal.

to reader demands. Above all, it is a story of great commercial success; of having the right idea at the right time, and the business nous to recognise it.

Along the way, it is also a tale of bitter rivalries, buying off competitors and demonstrating shrewd and cut-throat business instincts that would have served them just as admirably today. James Chalmers would not have taken long to find his feet in, then dominate, the Scottish media community two and a half centuries later.

JAMES CHALMERS is described in many learned histories as an Aberdonian, but he was nothing of the sort. He was a Moravian, born and bred. His father was minister at Dyke, three miles west of Forres, and the infant James was baptised there in 1713. He was 15 before he set foot in Aberdeen, when his father was transferred to a dual charge as minister of Greyfriars Kirk and Professor of Divinity at Marischal College.

Details of the early life of young James are sketchy, and many are uncorroborated, but we know that he was bright, articulate and musical, and could have chosen any of a number of careers. With so many doors open to him, quite why his family chose to make him an apprentice printer is uncertain.

In the middle of the 18th century, printing was regarded as more prestigious than a trade, certainly, but it fell well short of the cachet of a profession. The likeliest explanation is that Chalmers sen. had his mind on material, not spiritual, matters when he chose James's career, reasoning that printing would be a happy compromise between the status of a profession and the money of a trade. The Chalmers family might have become part of Aberdeen society, but a minister's stipend was far from handsome in the middle of the 18th century, even when bolstered by a professor's allowances, and any contribution from young James might have made all the difference between penury and comfort.

We don't know how much say James had in his career choice, but he was duly apprenticed to the only printer in Aberdeen, James Nicol. Mr Nicol had a happy and lucrative monopoly. He printed all the material for the town council and for Marischal College and must have been one of the most affluent businessman of his day.

James served his time and, like other apprentices of the era, normally would have stayed with his employer and worked his way through the firm. But ambition must have burned deep. Within months of finishing his apprenticeship in 1734, he left for London, where he felt he could develop his skills even further. Once there, he signed on as a junior printer with the firm of Watts, Lincoln's Inn Fields, a house specialising in legal work.

We know nothing more of James Chalmers until two years later. In 1736, he received a note in London telling him that his old boss in Aberdeen was gravely ill and was not expected to last the month.

Taking what seems now like an immense gamble, James resigned his post and headed north, ostensibly to pay his respects but, as we know now, with opportunity on his mind.

Within days of James's arrival, Mr Nicol had accepted that his own health was irreparable; had terminated his firm's city and college printing contracts voluntarily, and was preparing to wind up his business.

With commendable opportunism, on the same day, James Chalmers presented himself at the Town Chambers and applied to be permitted to succeed Mr Nicol. We cannot know if the baillies were amused, bemused or aghast at the boldness of the minister's son, or simply grateful that a problem had been followed so quickly by an obvious solution. In any case, James left the chambers with a fresh contract. Permission had been granted. At the age of 23, he was Official Printer to the Town Council of Aberdeen.

There is no record of how James conducted his business in those early years, although the fact that his annual contract was renewed without competition or question for at least the next 12 years speaks of high regard and growing status within the city.

Perhaps emboldened by this status, Printer Chalmers set himself to printing occasional bulletins, little more than single-sheet bills. None survives, but since James was a rabid Royalist and an opinionated fellow, it is safe to assume that his bulletins would have satisfied both traits admirably.

We know, for instance, that Jacobites were none too pleased with the Chalmers line. When a party of Prince Charlie's raiders occupied the town in November, 1745, one of their first calls was at the printer's office, which they raided on November 14.

A minister in Aberdeen, the Rev John Bisset, recorded in his journal of November 22:

> *Poor Chalmers, the printer, is from home, not yet able to walk with his strained leg he got jumping a window to escape the ruffians. They have committed great outrages in his house, breaking open an outer door when not let in,*

setting fire to an inner door and, when let in, scattering his types, searching his house, burning papers and breaking presses and drawers.

A second version of this story — which repetition has made almost historical truth — has it that the raiding Jacobites were fleeing after Culloden, and were wreaking revenge for a Chalmers report of the battle, but this is nonsense. Mr Bisset's diary dates are perfectly distinct.

In any case, the few Jacobites who escaped Culloden escaped in not more than twos and threes, certainly not a massed rank enough to occupy a town. Besides, it is doubtful that Royalist Aberdeen would have been a logical refuge for fleeing supporters of the Young Pretender.

There is also a tale which develops and embellishes the undoubted truth of Printer Chalmers leaping from his window. The story goes that he ran in fits, starts and hirples towards the Bridge of Dee where he sought shelter in what he had thought was a deserted outhouse. When his eyes had become accustomed to the gloom, he saw, staring back at him, a band of Jacobites, themselves in hiding until nightfall. They treated limping Chalmers kindly, for they had no idea who he was. We can imagine the printer's

NUMB. I

THE

ABERDEEN's JOURNAL

From TUESDAY December 29 1747, to TUESDAY January 5 1748

From the London Gazette, December 22.

Hamburgh, December 19. N. S.

THE Accounts which we receive of the late Hurricane are full of many disastrous Effects; of 30 Sail of Ships, which were lying in the Road of Cuxhaven, two only escaped either perishing, or being driven a shore. It was feared that the Boat belonging to His Britannick Majesty's Ship the Sheerness was lost, and the Men in her; but she was driven some Miles up a Creek, and received no Damage. A Dutch Officer is arrived here to inlist Volunteers for the Land-Service of the States-General; and their Minister in this Circle has applied for, and obtained Leave of the Magistrates for that Purpose.

Hague, Decr. 22. N. S. We are now informed from Zealand, that two Dutch Armed Vessels, of 20 Guns each, were lost near Flushing in the Storm of the 12th inst. and that not one of the Men were saved. The Dutch Officers, who were taken Prisoners of War by the French and have had Leave to come home upon their Parole, are greatly alarmed with a Declaration of M. Chiquet, that his Court intends shortly to order them all back again to France. The new Council of War has wrote circular Letters to all the General Officers in the Service of the State, who were employed at Bergen-op-Zoom, or in the Neighbourhood of that Place, to desire they would give in Writing whatever they know with any Certainty relating to the Defence of that Fortress. M. d'Envie, Major-General in the Bavarian Troops in this Country, arrived here three Days ago, in order to enter as Lieutenant-General into the Dutch Service.

Hague, Decr. 26. N. S. The Prince of Orange received last Saturday the solemn Deputation from the States of Overyssel, with the Diploma of his Election as Hereditary Stadtholder of that Province, and at the same Time His Highness took the Oaths proper upon that Occasion. The same Day it was publickly declared, that her Royal Highness the Princess of Orange was seven Months gone with Child. And Prayers have accordingly been ordered in all the Churches for her happy Delivery. The States of Holland, who have been constantly assembled for several Months, separated last Saturday for the Holidays, and are to resume the Assembly on the 10th of next Month. Before they separated, they resolved upon raising Four Millions Three hundred Thousand Florins by Way of Lottery, which is to be opened the 22d of next Month. Their High Mightinesses have lately published a Placart for the Encouragement of Privateers, by which they are not only to be exempted from the Obligation of giving up one Man out of Three for the Use the Fleet, but are likewise promised, upon taking any of the French Men of War or Privateers, a Reward of 150 Florins for every Man alive before the Engagement, and likewise the same Reward for every Pound Weight of Bill, computing together the Weight of Metal that each Gun carries on board the said Ships And as farther Encouragement, all Men of War, Privateers and other Ships thus taken, are to belong absolutely to the Captors, without any Deduction whatsoever. We hear from Paris that the Dragoons of Puygnyon, who have been for two Years past in Brittany, have received Orders to march the Beginning of the Spring for Flanders. Letters from Brussels of 20th mention, that Marshal Saxe set out for Paris the Sunday before, and Marshal Lowendahl at the same Time for Namur: and that the Marquis of Contadez[?], Governor of that City, commands there in the Absence of Marshal Saxe.

Admiralty-Office, Decr. 22.

Commodore Mostyn has sent into Plymouth the Grand St. Juan of St. Sebastian, a Privateer of 20 Guns, and 220 Men, which he took on the 7th inst. And also the Thetis of Bayonne, of 18 Guns, and 245 Men which he took on the 9th inst.

From the London Evening Post, December. 24.

Genoa, Dec. 9. The 2d Instant four Vessels arriv'd in our Harbour with some Corsican and and French Recruits: They fail'd from Calvi in Corsica the 26th of last Month in Company with 36 Ships more, which had on Board 1500 French and Spanish Troops, and steer'd for the Gulph of Spezzia. We have since receiv'd Advice that they are all safely landed at Porto-Fino, Sestri, and other Ports in this State.

Paris, Dec. 22. Marshal Saxe reckons to spend a Fortnight or three Weeks at Court, during which he is to assist at the Councils to be held on the new Measures that are to be pursued with respect to Military Operations in the Netherlands. As it is resolv'd that the War shall be carried on there with the utmost Vigour, the Court is making the necessary Dispositions for employing three Armies in that Country, viz. one of 60,000 Men is to assemble on the Meuse as soon as the Weather permits; another of the same Force will rendezvous near Bergen-op-Zoom; and the third Army is to be formed in the Neighbourhood of Louvain, in order to serve to reinforce either of the other two, as Occasion may require: Besides which, there is to be a Flying Camp, consisting of the light-arm'd Troops, which will be posted nearer to the Enemy's Frontiers. For the Execution of these Measures a Train of Artillery is getting ready in the Neighbourhood of Namur, which is to consist of 120 Pieces of Battering Cannon, and 40 Mortars, and we are to have another Train at Mechlin. Marshal Lowendahl is charged with the Direction of such Operations as are to precede the Opening of the Campaign in Form. Such are our Preparations for the Land Service, in the Midst of which we do not neglect the Marine. We are told the King has granted the Privateers[?] of St. Malo the Exemption from the Admiralty Fees and Duties which they had been following for some Time past; in Consideration[?] of which they engage to send out a greater Number of Ships than they have ever yet done. The Jews in this Kingdom have offer'd his Majesty to arm one hundred Ships of Force at their own Charge, if he will but give them Leave to build a Synagogue in this Metropolis: And Letters from Brest advise that the Jews are actually building there, as also at Rochefort, and some other adjacent Ports, twelve Men of War, which are to be ready against the Spring; and that the King is to pay them the Interest of their Money, 'till he can reimburse them the whole Expence of this Armament.

Paris, Dec. 25 The Comptroller of the Finances sent not long ago for the Farmers General, and told them his Majesty expected they should pay the Prizes in the present Lottery as fast as they were drawn: Upon this they express'd some Reluctance, and desired to have some Time to draw up their Remonstrances. The Comptroller told them, That as for Time it was precious; and as for Remonstrances, they would be vain; the King had already considered the Point, and would be obeyed; but added, That the King did not desire to constrain them, since there were others content to take their Farm upon themselves, and who, to obtain it, would do this and more.

Hague, Dece. 19. We have some private Letters from Hamburgh, which say, That the Great Mogul has entred Persia with an Army of 300 000 Men.

As the Publick may be alarmed with the Report that ran so currently Yesterday upon the Exchange, that a Contract is negociating for the Delivery of 400 000 Quarters of Wheat to our mortal Enemy the French, we hope every *Englishman* will judge so tenderly of his Neighbour, as not to believe it possible any Merchant can entertain so pernicious a Thought, or be such a Traitor to his Country, at a Time when our Allies the Dutch have totally prohibited all Commerce with that perfidious Nation under the severest Penalties.

However the Report Yesterday might arise, of a *particular Contract* for sending 400 000 *Quarters of Wheat* to France, it is certain that an Article from Bourdeaux, in a late Dutch Mail, mentions that a *large Number of English Ships*, laden with *Corn*, had put in there, and caused a sudden *Plenty* in the Midst of Scarcity; adding, that these Ships had failed under a *Pretence* of being bound for the *Mediterranean*. If these were *private Traders* only, who ventured thus to risk their *Fortunes*, in contempt of their *Duty* and *Allegiance*, the the Affair deserves to be particularly *enquired into*, that the Delinquents, if taken, may be *punished*. But if their Voyage was in Virtue of a *Contract*, that is a JOBB, the Business is the more *iniquitous*, as it must be a Transaction among Persons of *no small Distinction*. We will not pretend to guess who the JOBBERS may be; but it was very imprudent of the *French*, who were to be *essentially served*, to *blab a Secret* that may prevent their *Friends here* from making a little *more Profit* of our *present Plenty*.

We hear that it having been affirmed, in a certain *H------ Assembly*, that the Practice of *Sm-----g* would never have arisen to its *late Pitch* but for the Encouragement of some *R*—

Issue No.1 of the Aberdeen's Journal cost 1d and amounted to a single sheet folded in half to create four pages each measuring 9in. x 12in. The only illustration was the Bon Accord woodblock at the start of Page One.

flash of panic when one of the soldiers asked: 'And what's that bastard Chalmers up to now?'

'Still printing his Royalist manifestos,' said Chalmers, showing great presence of mind.

At that, some of the clansmen are supposed to have dropped to their knees and sworn on drawn dirks that if ever they clapped eyes on the printer, they would cut his throat.

On such romance is Hollywood fuelled.

There is no doubt, though, that Chalmers printed many and various anti-Jacobite bills. Neither is there any reason to doubt that he was at the Battle of Culloden itself for, by that time, he was not just the city printer but a man of trusted position in several spheres of city life.

A century later, his grandson gave a speech at a centenary dinner and told the assembly that Printer Chalmers had fought with the Duke of Cumberland's men at Culloden. There is no other proof of this, but it would not be too far-fetched to suppose that he had been sent as an observer by the city fathers, with instructions to report with all haste.

All haste in 1746 meant a day-and-a-half horse ride from Inverness to Aberdeen. Not only did James Chalmers report to the city fathers that the Jacobites had been routed and that a most bloody battle had been fought, he found the time to write up his observations and print another bill for public consumption. This was the first eye-witness account of a battle in Scottish newspaper history. In many ways, Chalmers was Scotland's first war correspondent.

The bulletin's public reception was rapturous. The Chalmers press could barely keep up with demand; never before had Aberdeen been accustomed to such hot news. More important, never before had Chalmers seen such hunger for information. We can imagine what was turning in his mind as he watched his work being read eagerly by the crowds of fellow-citizens thronging outside his office.

The obvious course was barred to him, for the city appointed him Official Receiver of various estates in Aberdeenshire that had been forfeited in defeat at Culloden. These duties occupied him for more than a year while his employees carried on with the day-to-day printing business, but by September, 1747, his official work was done and he was free to explore other avenues.

He knew the great risks and responsibilities in committing himself to publishing a regular newspaper, but his imagination had been fired during his two years in London and, since his return to Aberdeen, he had long been frustrated by the lack of regular information from the battle fronts abroad and from the royal court.

He must have known, also, that the market was untried north of Edinburgh. The Forbes family had published a pale newssheet in the mid-1660s, but not regularly and with little success.

Chalmers had few points of reference, then, as he and his wife, Susannah, discussed whether or not the time had come for a bold move. Ultimately, they agreed.

The town printer would become the town newspaper publisher.

THE first issue of *The Aberdeen's Journal* appeared on January 5, 1748, and was printed in a building just behind what is now the back wall of the Clydesdale Bank in Castle Street. The paper amounted to nothing more than a single sheet, folded in half to produce four pages. It had no headings, and the only relief from the tedium of three-column small type was the Bon Accord crest at the top left of the front page.

Unfortunately, there are no records of the circulation Chalmers achieved with his brainchild, but city historians have suggested that 500 sold copies would be near the mark. Since the paper cost a penny, the gross income from Issue No.1 was all of £2 and a few coppers.

The debut issue was not a typical local newspaper; it contained no local news whatsoever. Its entire content was lifted from the London papers of Christmas 1747, and so gave readers of the first issue little more than reports from the battle fronts of Europe.

The only Aberdeen content was the solitary advertisement:

On the 29th of last month went a-missing three promissory notes of the Aberdeen Company, one for £10 and two for 20s. each; and of the Bank of Scotland two for twenty shillings. Whoever brings them to the publisher of this paper shall have two guineas reward, and no questions asked.

There must have been little response, for the notice was repeated the following week.

The third issue is remarkable for containing the first reader's letter, a reply to a story in the previous week's paper which had announced that English corn was being sent to Bordeaux to feed the starving French.

The letter is long, windy and wordy (how little changes), but the gist of it gives a fascinating picture of xenophobia in 1748.

picture of xenophobia in 1748. It's amusing, too, that the first outraged opinion expressed in 250 years of the newspaper was that of an Englishman. The punctuation and capitalisation were of the time:

SIR—As an Englishman and as a sincere lover of my Native Country, I hope the rumour of corn-selling to the French is really such. Will not such Famine greatly reduce and enfeeble the army of the French, our mortal enemies, which has hitherto been formidable merely from it's superiority in numbers; and thus by bringing it to an Equality with our own and that of our Allies, give us victory over them in battle?

As providence has thought fit to afflict the French with so dreadful a scourge, may not the running counter to this benevolent Dispensation with regard to this Island turn that Blessing into a Curse?

Sir,

Yours,

FRUMENTARIUS

But James Chalmers got the measure very quickly of what the grass-roots North-east public wanted. By No.3, he had begun to include local news. The single column, which was headed from No.20 onwards:

DOMESTICK OCCURRENCES

contained reports of ship movements, mostly for lack of corroborated news from city and county, but other items in succeeding weeks paint far more more interesting pictures of the 1740s North-east life.

DOMESTICK OCCURRENCES

1. Last week, a Shop in Olddeer was broke open and robbed of Goods to a considerable Value, by some Rogues, who made off with their Booty undiscovered.

2. On Monday se'ennight some Thieves broke into the House of one Janet Symmers in Parish of Tarves, while the Family were asleep abed, and stole from thence 37s 3d Sterl., which was the poor Womans All.

3. On Tuesday, Alexander Carr in Parish of Upper-Banchory, being in Liquor, fell over the Bridge near Oldmiln, by which he was so much hurt, that he could only crawl a few Yards from the Place, when he instantly expired. And tho' he has no Relations that we know of; yet having above 30 l. Sterl., there soon appeared as many Friends as took Care to give the fellow a decent burial at his own Expence.

4. On Monday last, the following melancholy accident happened in Elgin. As William Fraser merchant was about to load a pistol to shoot a mad dog who bit Peter Anderson dyster, and was proving the flint, a spark caught hold of a cask of about 50 pounds of gunpowder, which drove out the forewall of the house with great violence and rendered the shop into a heap of rubbish.

James Grant, a taylor, and Laurence Calder, being below stair, were driven to the other side of the street, and were both killed. John Buy, a mainman, walking up the street, was by the force of a stone knocked down and killed. James Findlay, tho' in the shop when the accident happened, was only singed, and the flesh of his leg much torn. John Adam a grave-digger, and an apprentice of Peter Anderson, are most miserably hurt, and 'tis thought one Ross, a chapman, can not live.

But what is most remarkable in this case is, that William Fraser's wife, lying in bed in the part of the house off from the shop, was tossed up to the top of the room and received no other hurt, and a young girl at work in a window received a great shock but was no otherwise affected.

The windows of the adjacent houses suffered confiderable damage by the explosion, having their gaits and casements broken.

5. On Sunday Forenoon, two Children, one of three Years of Age, and the other, not quite so old, went into a planted Inclosure on the Tyrebagger, where they wandered for some Time. The eldest found the Way home, but the other, tho' searched for by a great Number of People, was not heard of yesterday morning.

The third issue is notable for the first property advertisement — offering the let of a croft at Mill of Bourty, Oldmeldrum, which was apparently specialised in 'dying, waulking and dressing cloaths' — and for broadening the range of goods and services advertised.

It did not take the North-east public long to appreciate the benefits of advertising. As winter gave way to spring, then summer, advertisements for cloth-bleaching, laundry, quack medicines, livestock, grazing and candlemaking appeared in increasing number.

Also in No.3, we have the paper's first missing-person appeal, for an Army deserter from Banff:

James Donald, aged 23 Years of Age, and five Foot six Inches and half high, by Trade a Shoemaker, who inlisted voluntarily in the Service of the States of Holland, under the Command of Ensign Roderick Mackdonald, and was duly attested the 4th of this Month, has been amissing for some time. If he returns to his Officer within eight Days after the Date of this he shall be forgiven and well used; but if not, shall be accounted as a Deserter; and any person who apprehends him, so that he may be brought to Ensign Mackdonald, or Ensign Lewis Chalmers at the Printing office, shall have a Reward of 20s.

N.B. He was born in Banff, has duskish Hair, a Cut on his right Eye-brow, and when he went away wore a blue Coat and Tartan Vest.

By No.28, published on July 12, 1748, the range of services advertised has broadened even further, and we have the first Lonely Hearts notice:

Any well-behaved young woman between thirty and fifty years of age, and having an hundred pounds at her own disposal, may, by directing a letter to O.Z. hear of an affable and agreeable husband of thirty-three.

And No.45, on November 8, 1748, offered the first correction:

The reader is desired to take notice that the Sale of William Logan's Goods was wrongly inserted, as to date, it beginning on Monday, November 14th.

As well as a rather alarming story from Buchan:

By Account from Peterhead, Fraserburgh, Etc, we hear there has been great Numbers of Locusts, and about this Town also; but as the Season is so far advanced, we hear of no Damage.

And an advertisement intended to appeal to those contemplating a new life in the New World:

James Gray, Merchant in Aberdeen, will set out for Virginia betwixt and the 20th of February next. This

Contemporary painting of Aberdeen across the River Dee

is therefore advertising all kinds of Tradesmen and Others that by applying to the said James Gray, any who has a mind to go abroad for a few Years will meet with better encouragement than has been formerly given.

NB: A proper person either in town or in country that will be at the Trouble to engage servants by applying to the said James Gray will be handsomely rewarded.

Such was the mix in the first year of the Aberdeen's Journal. As 1748 became 1749, James Chalmers must have been congratulating himself on a publication which had become popular, informative, indispensable and controversial in equal measure — an elusive mix which remains the ambition of every editor 250 years later.

His first year had been a process of trial and error; responding to public comment and complaint, treading warily and testing the the hunger and taste for news. As a result, Issue No.53 is markedly different in content to No.1. The advertising content (*2s 6d for the first time, and 2s for each time afterwards*) is what a modern managing director would describe as 'healthy', and all the more remarkable for having been sold despite the Government's hefty tax on all advertising.

No circulation figure is recorded, but a sale in the low four figures would seem near the mark, given the population of the North-east counties (10,000) and Aberdeen (9,000) at the time.

At any rate, Mr Chalmers was sufficiently pleased with the Journal's public reception that in his New Year issue for 1749, he was moved to verse:

My grateful thanks for all your favours past
Which pray continue this year as the last
From every post impartial I will cull
Whatever is not trifling, false or dull;
And though no more you must expect to hear
Of cities stormed or castles blown in air
The fruits of peace, of concord and of joy
And happier events shall press employ.

The hope for peace and better news in the new year is not terribly far removed from the sentiments of Hogmanay leaders in the Press and Journal of 250 years later.

By the end of the Aberdeen's Journal's first 12 months, the format was more or less established and, with minor adjustments over the succeeding 10 years, the paper had bedded down better than James Chalmers could have hoped.

The extraordinary thing to modern readers and journalists is how far-sighted Chalmers was in the mix of his newspaper and how similar that mix remains in the papers of today. The basic recipe was being followed 250 years ago. Only a lack of resources, technology and manpower prevented Chalmers from doing more.

By the middle of the 1750s, local news had taken priority over Continental wars and foreign dispatches, although it took second place to any story of national importance with regional implications. Each page is leavened with at least one, usually two, lighter items to brighten the gloom of war, death and disaster.

Typical was an item printed in 1759:

On the 2nd of this month a very extraordinary sight was seen at Cirton le Moor in Cumberland. A man, his wife and thirty of their children walking to the christening of their thirty-first. The youngest of the walkers was two years and five months old.

Few newspapers today would not use such a story on Page One, given the chance.

There was also the tale of a Keith woman who had dressed as a man in order to enlist.

A young girl has drest herself in men's apparel for the purpose to enlist as a Royal Volunteer, for which she received four guineas as bounty money. She made her escape from the barracks that night, with her bounty. Being discovered in a day or two, she was obliged to return her gains.

And a story which would not have been amusing at the time to the apprentice carpenter involved, but the tone of the reporting suggests that Mr Chalmers, and probably many readers, could see a funny side:

Some hecklers, being in their cups, persuaded a young beginner in their business at his head-washing that it was absolutely necessary for him to be initiated into their pretended Mysteries, and to undergo some indis-

pensable Ceremonies before he could be admitted into the Fraternity. The simple lad having consented, they bedaubed his head and face all over with pitch and tar, overlaid it with tallow and poured on brandy over all. They then set the whole on fire, which scorched the poor fellow so miserably that for some time his life was despaired of.

It is around this time that we can sense a growing public spirit in Editor Chalmers. With more than a year of successful publication behind him, he feels emboldened to speak on behalf of less well-educated, humbler souls in his readership. But he does it in an early form of satire. To put it in context, we'll look at a public notice printed at the request of the Kirk Session at Keith. Editor Chalmers accepted the notice (it was revenue, after all) but, as we shall see, was horrified by the intolerance and hypocrisy of supposed Christians.

Advertisement

By Appointment of the Kirk-Session of Keith

That whereas one Elspet Sellar, an unmarried Woman in this Parish, was convicted before this Kirk-Session, upon a Delation of her being with Child in Uncleanness, but denied. Sometime after the Report becoming more frequent, and the Neighbours affirming, she had all Symptoms of a Woman with Child, and from her Conduct, suspecting she had very bad Intentions, was again summoned before the Session, but in the mean time she made an Elopement. The last notice of her was at Huntly. She is of low stature, black Complexion, hath a Burthen of Cloths with her, wore a white Plaid marked E.S, is about Thirty Years of Age. It is earnestly recommended to the several ministers and Kirk Sessions to make diligent Enquiry within their respective parishes for discovering her and detecting her Wickedness, and discouraging the like Practices in others.

John Gilchrist Minr.

We'll never know if poor Elspet Sellar was discovered and punished, but the issue struck home with Editor Chalmers. A few issues later, he published a supposed Question and Answer dialogue between an ardent believer in the rigid Christianity of the day, supposedly deceased and now safe in Heaven, and an Earthbound innocent seeking answers to questions of religion which were troubling him. It was a straight lift from a French paper circulating in America at the time, but the subtext is clear.

Q. How is the Soil made in Heaven?
A It is a very fair Soil; they want neither for Meats nor Cloaths. 'Tis but wishing and we have them.

Q. Are they employed in Heaven?
A No. They do nothing; the Fields yield the Corn, Pumpkins, and the like, without any Tillage.

Q. What sort of Trees are there growing in the fields of Heaven?
A. Always green, full and flourishing.

Q. Have they in Heaven the same Sun, the same Wind, the same Thunder we have here?
A The Sun ever shines. 'Tis always fair Weather.

Q. How are their Fruits?
A. In this one Quality they exceed ours, that they are never wasted; you have no sooner plucked one than you see another hanging in its Room.

Q. What Sort of Soil is that of Hell?
A. A very wretched Soil. 'Tis a fiery Pit in the Centre of the Earth.

Q. Have they Light in Hell?
A. No. 'Tis always dark; there is always Smoke, with which their eyes are always in Pain; they can see nothing but Devils.

Q. What shaped things are the Devils?
A. Very ill-shaped Things, they go about with Vizards on, and they terrify Men.

Q. What do they eat in Hell?

A. They are always hungry, but the Damned feed on hot Ashes and Serpents there.

Q. What water have they to drink?

A. Horrid water; nothing but melted lead.

Q. Don't they die in Hell?

A. No. Yet they eat one another every Day, but anon God restores and renews them that were eaten, as a cropt Plant in a little Time shoots out.

Printing such a tract was infinitely more audacious in a small town in the middle of the 18th century than it would be in these sceptical times.

Not only that, but it was printed by a man of great influence in the city, who moved in the most exalted and professional circles, clergy included, and who was himself a minister's son.

There is no record of Kirk reaction to the tract, but we can guess. And it is yet further proof that Chalmers was his own man.

By the end of 1749, we have first-hand evidence of how well the paper was selling, for James Chalmers penned his second New Year message to his readers. The language is archaic to modern eyes, but the sentiment is not:

Two years have now passed since this paper was first published and, as it has always been my study to avoid giving offence to any person or party, the crying demand for it flatters me of its kindly reception by the public who now have an opportunity of being served with the most material, occurrences, foreign and domestic, of the whole week at an easy rate.

If in some paragraph appears from what may be called a party paper, let it be considered that there is a difference between author and publisher, that the liberty of the press shows us to be a free people, and has often been found a check upon those in power; and sometimes complaints without doors have had a very happy influence on councils within.

So Editor Chalmers had distinct views on the freedom of the Press.

Considering that his contract as printer to the Town depended on good relations with the council, he was a decidedly brave man to publish regular criticism of the authorities who awarded him the bulk of his business.

Only once did he fall from grace. A trades convener in Aberdeen, saddler James Smith, had stated publicly that a former Provost, Alexander Livingstone, of Countesswells, was part of a cartel responsible for inflating the price of meal, and that citizens were suffering as Livingstone lined his pockets.

The Journal, sensing another slight against the suffering masses, duly printed the attack. But Livingstone sued Smith and won. Smith was called to attend the bar and apologise in person to Livingstone. He did this and was admonished.

Chalmers, however, had no such easy retreat. He had published Smith's words in full, and Livingstone wanted reparation for having been mocked and accused 'abroad and in publick'.

The result of what was, loosely, Scotland's first newspaper-libel action was the burning of a copy of the offending paper at the gallows by the town hangman before as large a crowd as Livingstone could muster.

In a foretaste of the modern Press Complaints Commission, the Editor was also required to print a public retraction in his next issue, which he did readily.

What was inserted in this paper of the 23rd inst., as publisher of the Aberdeen Journal I hereby acknowledge was rash and indiscreet. I am now satisfied that what was inserted with respect to the meal retailers was a false representation of the true facts; and that the paper given and printed by me in the paper of the ninth inst. was an untrue account of the affair between Provost Livingstone and J. Smith and printed by me in the Journal of the twenty-third current, which was, by sentence of the magistrates yesterday, publicly burned by the hands of the common hangman.

It was a deeply embarrassing episode for one of Aberdeen's leading citizens, an Editor who had prided himself on accuracy and successful defence of the public interest.

But Chalmers learned his lesson. He was not stung twice.

YEARS passed and James Chalmers adjusted the content of his newspaper to stay in tune with public taste. Within four years, the apostrophe had been dropped from the Aberdeen in the titlepiece and the paper had become simply *The Aberdeen Journal*.

At some stage, he seems to have decided that the way to maximise readership was to appeal to as many different trades and professions as possible, for he began including agricultural news, news for fishermen, news for dominies and news for the businesspeople of town and county.

This is not so far removed from the specialists' desks at the modern Press and Journal.

His agricultural section printed letters from farmers. On January 17, 1759, he published the thoughts of one unidentified crofter doing his best to survive a famine, and offering advice for others in the same predicament:

SIR: As you communicate to the publick hints for their advantage, please recommend to them in your next Journal to use beat whinns and cut tops of heather, mixed with other food, for horses; and heather-tops and sea-ware for black cattle, to supply, in some degree, the present scarcity of provender.

Or, as is now done in the Lothians, may use clean potatoes, cut in very small pieces, for the horses, and the same a little boiled for cows.

Some may also presently sow rye, upon which they may feed their cattle 'till the grass is up, and then turn down the rye for bear land.

I am,&c.

The Journal sold principally to the educated classes, obviously, for the heyday of Scottish education was yet to come. We can trace the growing appeal of the paper drifting from the trades to the professions by the number of advertisements intended to appeal to the middle and upper classes. Typical is one such notice appearing in early 1759:

Advertisement.

On Wednesday the 25th inst. there will be sold by auction, the Hebrew, Spanish and Arabic BOOKS, according to catalogue of last auction; — at the same time there will be added for sale, several very curious and valuable English books, pamphlets and maps. The sale to be in the Marischal College, and to begin precisely at 6 o'clock at night. The books, &c may be seen any day 'twixt and the time of sale, by applying to Alexander Angus.

It's an interesting example of the premium put on education in Aberdeen in the middle of the 18th century. Despite its two universities, Aberdeen was a small settlement, of little more than 20 streets and 10,000 residents. For such a place to be able to host an auction of learned works when only 20% of the population would have been literate is remarkable.

The same issue gives a more general flavour of those warlike times, with a notice encouraging able-bodied men to enlist to fight for King George II. The success of the little sweetener offered to persuade fathers to deliver their sons is not recorded.

Advertisement

All GENTLEMEN VOLUNTEERS who are able and willing to serve his Majesty King George in his Majesty's third regiment of foot guards, commanded by the right honourable John, earl of Rothes, and in the honourable captain Cosmo Gordon's company, let them repair to his recruiting serjeant at Old Meldrum, where any man 5 feet 8 inches, not exceeding 25 years of age or, 5 feet seven and one half inches high, and not exceeding 29 years of age, shall receive TWO GUINEAS bounty money, and a CROWN to drink his Majesty's health; and likewise from the date of their inlisting, Eight Pence per day subsistence. Whoever has a mind, must repair to Oldmeldrum, on or before Monday the 23rd inst.

N.B. Any person to bring a man as above to enlist shall receive half a guinea reward.

By the end of his fourth year, James Chalmers was a rich man, re-investing most of his profit in new type and a new press. Business was good — so good that others had begun to notice. They saw their chance to make money, too.

Chalmers would not enjoy his monopoly for much longer.

CHAPTER II

Spice of Competition

FRANCIS DOUGLAS and William Murray were two middle-ranking Aberdeen businessmen in the middle of the 18th century. Douglas had been a baker, but was an avid reader and had adapted his hobby into a lucrative sideline by opening a bookshop. Murray was one of the city's foremost druggists.

Both had watched the inexorable rise of Chalmers and his Daily Journal with a mixture of admiration and envy. Here was a man who had begun with virtually nothing, yet through little but his own labour, foresight and contacts had become one of the most influential men in the city. It seemed too important a prize to be left to one family.

Neither Douglas nor Murray had sufficient resources to mount a challenge as individuals, but when, by chance, they discovered their common ambition, they realised that, in partnership, they had the springboard they needed. With Murray's business contacts and finance and Douglas's self-taught skills with the written word, they founded the first rival paper to the Daily Journal. The Aberdeen Intelligencer appeared in October, 1752.

We don't know how James Chalmers and the Journal reacted, for there appears to be no mention of the new arrival in the Journal's columns. Neither does there seem to be any noticeable change in Journal content, cover price, advertising rate or editorial policy. Perhaps Chalmers was content to bide his time and not react overtly to his new competition.

Murray and Douglas, meanwhile, were shrewd enough to know that squaring up head on to the mighty Journal would guarantee early defeat. Instead, they decided that the likeliest market niche lay with a readership being ignored by the Journal. In the northern half of Scotland, that meant disgruntled Jacobites, who found little appeal in the Journal's staunch support of Whiggery.

So that was the editorial road

Robert Burns (left) meets James Chalmers II (right). Bishop John Skinner is seated centre. The encounter in the Daily Journal office in 1787 is recorded in the writings of all three men.

RIGHT: The grandfather clock which still keeps perfect time outside the Aberdeen Journals boardroom is almost as old as the Press and Journal. It was installed at the old Daily Journal offices in the Castlegate in 1769. Legend has it that Burns adjusted his own pocket-watch by it.

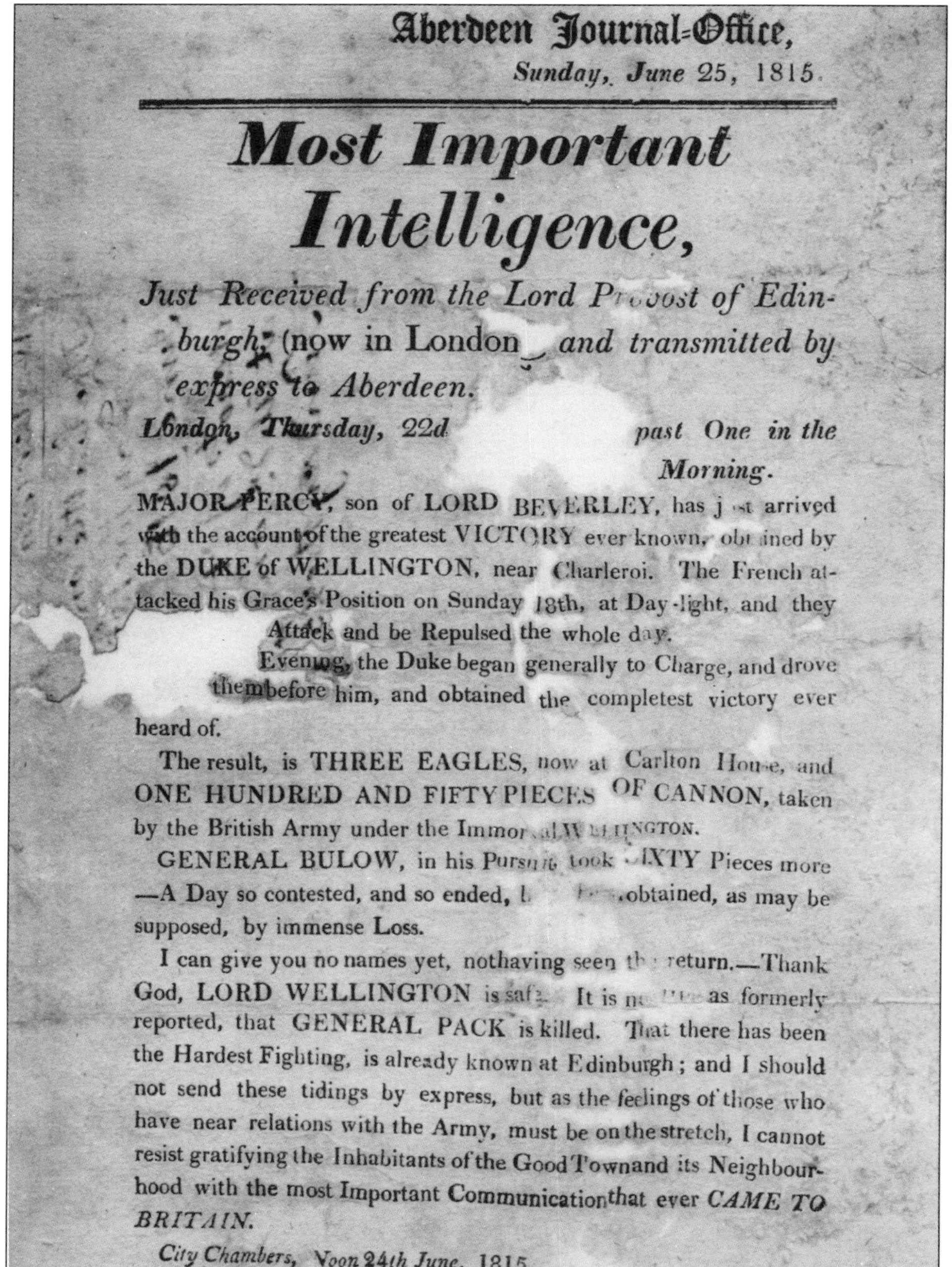

Aberdeen Journal-Office,
Sunday, June 25, 1815.

Most Important Intelligence,

Just Received from the Lord Provost of Edinburgh, (now in London) and transmitted by express to Aberdeen.

London, Thursday, 22d [illegible] *past One in the Morning.*

MAJOR PERCY, son of LORD BEVERLEY, has just arrived with the account of the greatest VICTORY ever known, obtained by the DUKE of WELLINGTON, near Charleroi. The French attacked his Grace's Position on Sunday 18th, at Day-light, and they [illegible] Attack and be Repulsed the whole day. [illegible] Evening, the Duke began generally to Charge, and drove them before him, and obtained the completest victory ever heard of.

The result, is THREE EAGLES, now at Carlton House, and ONE HUNDRED AND FIFTY PIECES OF CANNON, taken by the British Army under the Immortal WELLINGTON.

GENERAL BULOW, in his Pursuit took SIXTY Pieces more —A Day so contested, and so ended, [illegible] obtained, as may be supposed, by immense Loss.

I can give you no names yet, not having seen the return.—Thank God, LORD WELLINGTON is safe. It is not [illegible] as formerly reported, that GENERAL PACK is killed. That there has been the Hardest Fighting, is already known at Edinburgh; and I should not send these tidings by express, but as the feelings of those who have near relations with the Army, must be on the stretch, I cannot resist gratifying the Inhabitants of the Good Town and its Neighbourhood with the most Important Communication that ever *CAME TO BRITAIN.*

City Chambers, Noon 24th June, 1815.

The last surviving example of the special-edition news-sheet put out by the Journal to announce Wellington's victory at Waterloo.

FAR RIGHT: The Waterloo news-sheet was printed by hand on this Eagle press. This same press was still in use at Broad Street in the 1960s, when it was used to proof pages for sub-editors. Today, it has earned a dignified retirement at the Lang Stracht, testament to the workmanship of Georgian press engineers.

followed by the Intelligencer, and exceptionally successful they were. While papers were opened and shut down in matters of weeks and months throughout the rest of the country, in Aberdeen the Intelligencer bedded down for a long and successful stay. It lasted for almost five years.

Then, as now, inter-newspaper rivalries were rarely fought in the editorial pages, much as journalists would like to persuade themselves otherwise. Newspaper storms have always raged their wildest around the advertisements. Specifically, the paper which can deliver the most customers at least cost to advertising clients is the paper that earns the revenue and survives to pursue its editorial ambitions. Even 240 years ago, editorial rivalries and differences in tone mattered little compared to the need for finance.

And this was the Intelligencer's undoing.

In 1757, a meeting of the Commissioners of Supply for the County of Aberdeen, approached both proprietors to discuss a difficulty being faced by the authorities and businesspeople in the city and county. Simply, the cost of advertising in both papers was too great.

'If there was but one paper, those who had goods for sale and services for public appeal might thus save half the cost of advertisement,' suggested one commissioner.

As a result, Chalmers bought out Douglas and Murray, who were said to be glad to leave a notoriously difficult business. The Intelligencer was absorbed by its rival in February, 1757.

It was the only challenge that Chalmers had faced to his monopoly, and he had won.

Seven years later, on August 25, 1764, James Chalmers died. He was 51.

THE power vacuum that follows the death of any chairman or chief executive was no less pronounced at the Journal. Susannah Chalmers, the widow, had no experience in business, and what little she had learned of publishing she had learned in conversation with her husband.

Widow Chalmers must have had little time to mourn formally, considering the immense business pressures that had fallen about her. Taking stock showed her that, mercifully, she had few staff to look after, for most of the men who worked the printing machine were on contract from the Shore Porters Society. Distribution would present no problems, for that was handled by carriers and mail coaches. Advertising revenue would continue to arrive steadily.

The difficulty lay in producing and maintaining the editorial content, which had always been the sole province of her husband. Susannah knew that in the short term, at least, she could keep the paper ticking over by reverting quietly to her husband's early practice of lifting material from the London and Edinburgh papers. But readers would not tolerate that for long, now that they had become accustomed to local news, edited locally.

The key would be an experienced hand back on the tiller. She had not far to look. Her son, also James, was in a printing apprenticeship in London when his father died. After nine days of uncertainty, a notice appeared prominently on Page One of the Journal of September 3, 1764.

To the PUBLIC

As Mr Chalmers the late Publisher of this Journal died the 25th of last Month, Mrs Chalmers his Widow begs leave to acquaint the Public that her Son James, who was bred to the Printing Business with his Father, and for several Years past has been at London prosecuting and improving himself in his Business, designs soon to return to and to carry on his Business in this Place, in Conjunction with Mrs Chalmers his Mother, who in the mean Time keeps up the Business as formerly.

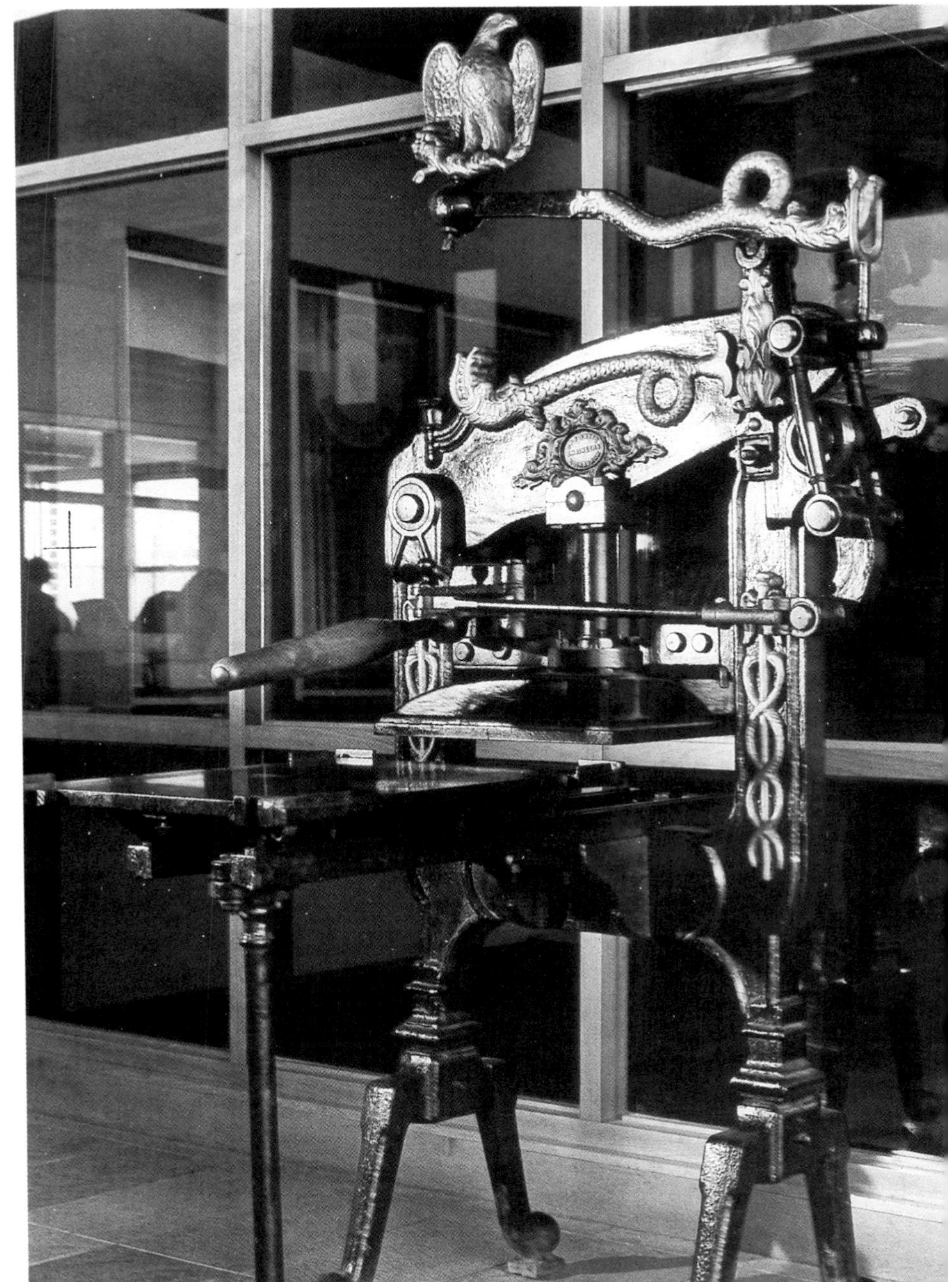

Mrs Chalmers thinks it her indispensible Duty to return her sincere Thanks to the Public, and particularly to all the Gentlemen in the Town and County of Aberdeen, for their many Favours shewn to her late Husband, and hopes for the Continuance of them, which if she obtain, she and her Son will always endeavour to execute them in such a Manner as may Merit their Continuance.

The Aberdeen Journal will be regularly published weekly as before, and Subscribers may depend that no Pains nor Expence will be spared in collecting such Intelligence and Occurrences as may render it both entertaining and useful.

Susannah Chalmers might not have been a businesswoman, but she was a shrewd student of human nature. Her prompt action spiked the guns of likely rivals; assured printing-contract clients that all was stable and well, and gave her son time to tidy his affairs in London before hurrying home to take control.

Businesspeople centuries later would have done pretty much the same in the circumstances.

JAMES the Second stamped his mark on the Aberdeen Journal with surprising speed and confidence, considering his youth (he was 23) and the long shadow of such a successful father.

He introduced new, smaller typefaces "so that the paper may contain more matter". He tidied the layout into sections so that readers might navigate it better. So doing, he was more than two centuries ahead of newspaper-design consultants who fly the globe today advising proprietors and editors on exactly the same thing and charging handsomely.

Being a student of Marischal College and Cambridge University, James had been well schooled to the arts, which must explain his decision to introduce arts coverage and promote Scots painters, poets and writers of the day with great vigour. Arts coverage did not always sit easily in the confines of a weekly newspaper so, in 1787 he tried a bold experiment by launching a second title.

His Northern Gazette and Literary Chronicle and Review of the Month was biased heavily to a learned readership and he was certain that it would succeed.

It was an abject failure. The experiment taught James a costly lesson: a publication whose market is not researched and assessed properly in advance is almost always doomed. His literary review folded after just eight months.

Chastened by the failed venture, James resolved instead to tinker with the recipe of the Journal. He changed publication day from a Tuesday to a Monday but, far more important, it is from the 1790s that we can date many of the innovations that are still current in today's Press and Journal.

In 1791, he dropped his intermittent editorial attacks on city standards and introduced in their place a regular statement of opinion, appearing in the same box on the same page almost every week. In effect, he introduced the leader, which survives in the modern Press and Journal as the daily Comment.

He introduced what contemporary journalists know as 'the colour piece', by which he reported a hot news topic of the time, then took space to explain the background issues in greater depth, usually presenting them in terms of a human story.

And, unwilling to abandon his beloved arts entirely, he introduced book reviews from 1793. He also introduced a cover-price increase — to 3½d. Innovations must be financed somehow.

It was perhaps this obsession with the arts and learning that brought James Chalmers his most celebrated visitor. In September, 1787, a 28-year-old poet from South-west Scotland arrived in Aberdeen and made his way up the Journal stairs, curious to meet Editor Chalmers.

RIGHT:
Inverness from Godsman's Walk in 1823. Around this time, the Journal began regular coverage of affairs in the Highland capital.

His name was Robert Burns. Burns carried little weight with the Aberdeen public; the Journal reported the visit only briefly:

Yesterday passed through Aberdeen on his return from a tour to the north Robert Burns, the celebrated Ayrshire bard.

For a record of the hour's conversation, we have to turn to one of the diaries which Burns kept, and even then details are sketchy:

'Came to Aberdeen. Met with Mr Chalmers, printer (a facetious fellow) . . . Aberdeen, a lazy town.'

The national bard was no more important in northern Scotland nine years later when the Journal reported his death decidedly curtly:

On the 21st inst. died at Dumfries, after a lingering illness, the celebrated poet Robert Burns.

Even five years later, when the Journal reported that the Burns birthplace had been converted into a public house, there was no adulation.

It took until 1814, when the Journal reported that the Old Bridge of Doon had been saved from demolition, for the status of Burns to become apparent:

It must give pleasure to the admirers of genius and polite literature to hear that the stigma which has so long attached to Scotland for neglecting to do honour to her native bard, Robert Burns, is about to be wiped away. A meeting was on Thursday last held in the George Inn, Dumfries, for the purpose of taking measures to erect a mausoleum over the remains of that extraordinary man.

James Chalmers II died in 1810. He had piloted the Journal for almost half a century. He had seen to it that Scots were kept abreast of news at one of the most profound periods of world history. His paper had reported American Independence, the French Revolution, the discovery of Australia, the Battle of Trafalgar and the abolition of slavery.

THE times were no calmer for his successor, his second son. David Chalmers was supposedly less intellectual than his father or grandfather, but he made up for his lack of flair with great industry. He read every item of news before publication, so jealous was he of the paper's reputation. And despite his supposed life in the shadow of his predecessors, it was David Chalmers who made the Aberdeen Journal the biggest

newspaper in Scotland. The stamp-duty returns of 1832 show that the Journal was selling 2,231 copies a week, ahead of the Edinburgh Weekly Journal (2,192), the Scotsman (1,914), the Glasgow Herald (1,615), the Dundee Advertiser (1,163), the Inverness Courier (615) and the Perth Advertiser (596). Spurred by the success, David Chalmers enlarged his paper to 12 pages weekly.

Perhaps this same success made him an easy target for would-be rivals. Once, he was challenged to a duel at the City Links by James Adam, editor of the rival Aberdeen Herald. David Chalmers' interest lay not in fighting, which he left to lesser men, but in his business. That showed itself most markedly by continual innovation. His interest in the birth of the machine age led him to convert the Journal's press to steam power in 1830, the first Scottish newspaper to do so.

He believed in change, and he believed that the best means of spiking the competition was by using new technology whenever it was available to him. When he stood before a celebration dinner in 1848 to mark his paper's centenary, he held aloft a copy of Issue No.1, the humble folded sheet that his grandfather had watched being bought so hungrily, and smiled.

'Sirs,' he told 200 councillors, businessmen, county gentlemen and academics, 'I am told by Mr Barclay of Knockleith that he has in his neighbouring parish a man of one hundred and four years; four years older than this publication which you kindly honour today. Having seen the first issue of the Journal, he informed Mr Barclay that it was "*jist lik twa leaves o a Bible*".'

Laughter erupted at once and, when David Chalmers sat down eventually, he received a lengthy standing ovation.

It was well-earned. Not just for the changes and improvements he had brought to north Scottish newspapers, but for the stoicism with which he saw off so much competition — far more than his father or grandfather had had to endure. Scarcely a year passed without a new title venturing on to the streets of Aberdeen Mostly, they came in the form of ill-planned amateur sheets, or secular newsletters too numerous to mention. Among them:

1825 North Briton
(*lasted three weeks*)

1826 Aberdeen Star
(*13 months*)

1829	Aberdeen Observer	*(eight years)*
1832	Aberdeen Pirate	*(one issue)*
1832	Scots Champion	*(one issue)*
1832	Aberdeen Pirate II	*(a year)*
1833	Aberdeen Mirror	*(a year)*
1834	Aberdeen Shaver	(five years)
1835	Aberdeen Advertiser	*(11 months)*
1840	Aberdeen Banner	*(11 years)*
1847	North of Scotland Gazette	*(six years)*

Only two are of any interest.

The Aberdeen Shaver was a monthly satirical magazine. It thrived on pricking the city authorities and did genuine investigative journalism. It laid bare a book-pricing cartel among all Aberdeen booksellers, railing at the price of knowledge.

It ran lengthy features warning Aberdonians to beware of quack doctors selling dubious cholera medicines.

It exposed the Aberdeen medical hierarchy's habit of drawing salaries at the Aberdeen General Dispensary, but sending students to do the work.

But vaulting ambition o'erleapt itself, and soon the Shaver had set itself up as moral guardian of the masses. In one celebrated edition it advised darkly that:

We have got notice of a scandalous practice carried on by several married women in a house in Carmelite Lane. We bid them beware, as we will make a call some of these dark evenings and report.

Reports such as these were its undoing, for it became embroiled in a series of punishing libel actions and went out of business in 1839.

The second was the 1847 launch of the North of Scotland Gazette. In itself, it was nothing extraordinary, with suspicions throughout the city that it lifted much of its news from the Journal, albeit reworded slightly. The Gazette did not assume its more ominous proportions until 1853 when, over the weekend of April 28/29, it transformed itself into the Aberdeen Free Press.

We cannot know if David Chalmers sensed that real competition had arrived at last, but it is curious that he watched the Free Press match the Journal closely in price, size, content and tone week by week and enjoy substantial leaps in circulation, and decided within the year to retire.

He was the first proprietor not to die in office, making over the management and editing of the Journal to his sons James and John Gray Chalmers. He died peacefully five years later in 1859.

THE two Journal editors tried to face down the competition as best they could but, in 1865, the Free Press launched a surprise attack.

It began publishing twice weekly.

James and John did not react; convinced that the market could not stand such saturation coverage, but they were wholly wrong. The novelty of twice-weekly news, far from wearing off quickly, took a strong grip of Aberdeen and the North-east.

James and John were wrong-footed yet again by biding their time while the Free Press grew ever more successful. Seven years later, the Free Press seized the initiative once more and began publishing daily.

This time, the Chalmers brothers had to react and, in May, 1876, they sold the paper, premises and plant to form the North of Scotland Newspaper and Printing Company Ltd. so that the Journal could afford to begin daily publication.

So began almost half a century of direct rivalry between the Liberal young upstart, the Free Press, and the Conservative old hand, the Daily Journal.

For more than 46 years, the Press and the Journal were to do battle to be first daily.

LEFT:
Inverurie en fête for an 1840s visit of the young Queen Victoria.

CAMPBELL

CHAPTER III

A Difficult Marriage

IN PURE news terms, the Press and the Journal joined battle at precisely the right time. The world was in flux and the pickings were rich for newspapers and their journalists. Among the stories covered by both papers were the collapse of the Tay Bridge, the founding of the Scottish Labour Party by Keir-Hardie, the exploits of Jack the Ripper, the opening of the Forth Bridge, the founding of the Scottish Trades Union Congress, the unveiling of the Statue of Liberty, the inception of the modern Olympic Games, the invention of powered flight by the Wright Brothers, the inventions of the internal-combustion engine and the motor-car, the introduction of moving pictures, the deaths of Gladstone and Queen Victoria, the Boer War, the suffragette movement, Captain Scott's ill-fated trip to the Antarctic, the shooting of Archduke Ferdinand in Sarajevo, the Quintinshill Rail disaster, the Easter Uprising in Ireland and, of course, the sinking of the Titanic.

Slow news days were rare for the rival news editors, as each matched the other punch for punch in breadth of regional, national and international coverage. To modern eyes, either paper is anything but parochial. The outlooks are cosmopolitan and global, and the tones of both are so uncannily similar that the competition must have been keen and unrelenting.

The Free Press's determination to blaze trails caused constant headaches for Journal editor William Forsyth. The Press expanded from four daily pages to eight, yet Forsyth could not persuade his board to follow suit and he saw his circulation drift to his rival.

So disgusted was he with his board's constant refusal to sanction extra pages that he resigned in early 1879, at virtually the same time as the Journal board revealed why they could not have afforded to expand his paper: they were launching a new ha'penny evening paper, to be called the Evening Express.

This time, it was the turn of the Free Press board to consider and react. Within months, they launched their answer to the Evening Express, the Evening Gazette.

Now, Aberdeen and the North of Scotland had four daily newspapers. Considering the population and education of the northern half of Scotland at the time, the market must have been beyond saturation. Ironically for the now-departed William Forsyth, the Evening Express was such a success that it generated enough reserve income to allow the board to expand the Journal to eight pages, three days a week. That began on July 4, just five months after Mr Forsyth had stormed from the building.

Alas, market saturation began to tell. Profits were thin in a newspaper market that then, as now, was volatile and vulnerable to the regional economy. With no real capital to speak of, the Journal went into liquidation in 1884. The firm reconstituted itself at once, which freed enough capital to allow a

LEFT

Union Street, Aberdeen, at its Edwardian best. Competition between rival newspapers throughout Scotland was intense — nowhere more than in the North and North-east.

Elgin celebrates the coronation of Edward VII. Communities throughout the North and North-east of Scotland arranged ceremonies which seem incredibly elaborate to modern eyes.

make-or-break pitch for the crucial and elusive increase in circulation — eight-page papers Monday to Saturday every week. Sadly, even that was not enough to satisfy the fickle paper-buying public. By 1886, the Journal circulation had fallen below 10,000 and the directors called an extraordinary general meeting to debate whether or not to shut it down and concentrate on the successful Evening Express.

They decided against closure, and raised money by inviting employees to purchase debentures. More strikingly, they asked that employees form a staff advisory committee to report to the board so that workers could feel that they had some say in their company. In effect, the Journal was at least a century ahead of the rest of the industry by introducing staff representation on the board.

The weakness of the Journal had not gone unnoticed outside the firm, however. In 1889, the Free Press offered to buy the title for £4,000. The Journal board turned down the offer. Happily, by that stage, losses had bottomed out and the paper was making a small profit. That profit, however, was pitifully small, at £236, certainly nowhere nearly enough to invest in the company and improve the building and printing plant.

Then an extraordinary thing happened.

The Journal board was convened for a special meeting in early November, 1890. In the corner sat the company's legal advisers. When invited to speak, one stepped forward to announce that John Gray Chalmers, the last surviving great-grandson of founder James Chalmers, had left the company £10,000 in his will, instructing his trustees and the company board to invest it in the Journal's future. Human spirits have rarely soared so high as they did in that small room that morning. The mood was so elated that the directors quite forgot that their salvation had come of death.

Within three years, they had bought premises in Broad Street, which accounted for more than half of their £10,000 legacy.

The first Broad Street papers were produced on May 19, 1894. As new technology developed, the company installed a private wire between the papers' London office and Broad Street. They installed three printing presses. Circulation began climbing. Advertising revenue became firmer. By 1895, the company made a £950 profit.

The following year saw a profit of £1,824 — enough to persuade the directors to abandon hand typesetting and to buy eight automatic Linotype machines. The Editor of the day, David Pressly, wrote later that the Linotypes were the single greatest advance a newspaper could have imagined and that his compositors were then able to process as much copy in a day as would have taken four months 50 years before.

In 1899, the company bought its first typewriter, so that secretaries might issue correspondence 'in a manner fitting professional newspaper publications'. Later the same year, the company asked Aberdeen Town Council for permission to advertise on the side of the Corporation trams. Permission was granted for £20 a year. In time for the start of the new football season, the Evening Express was authorised to begin a weekly football edition, the forerunner of the modern Green Final.

The company decided to establish its own delivery fleet, and signed contracts with the Webster Brothers joinery firm in Jopp's Lane to build three carts

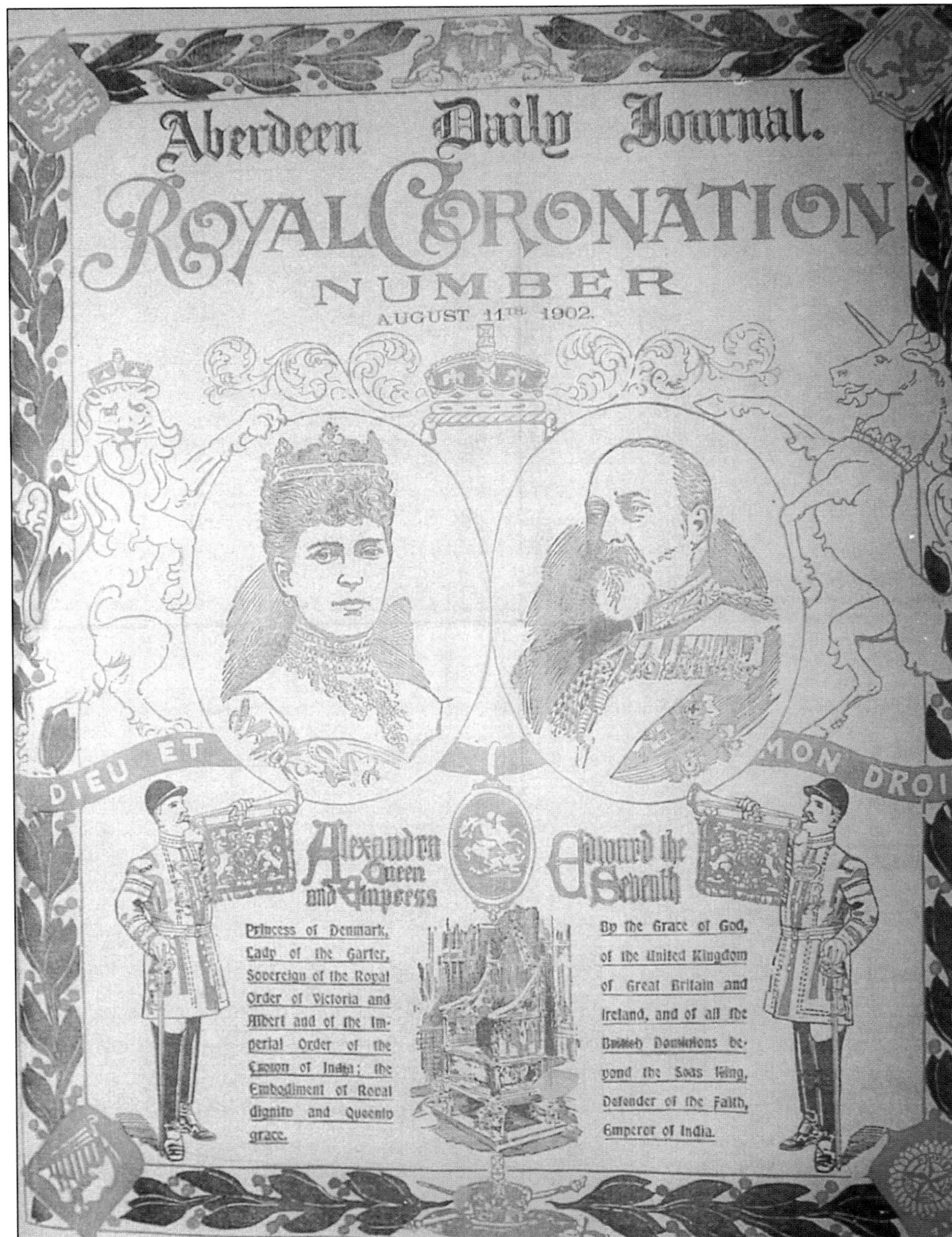

The 1902 Coronation number of the Daily Journal was the first three-colour paper printed in Aberdeen and involved a great many unpaid overtime hours.

Five of its 16 pages were printed in purple, chocolate and red, with shades of green and orange thrown in for good taste.

The company offered free souvenir wrappers for posting abroad.

So complicated was the exercise that printing in colour was not tried again until 1963.

'suited for horses of 15 hands, not to exceed 5ft in width'.

On August 9, 1902, the Journal produced the first colour newspaper in Scotland, to mark the coronation of Edward VII.

In 1908, the company hired a motor-car so that reporters could cover the campaigning for the general election.

In 1910, a new Editor was appointed. William Maxwell had worked on the London Evening Standard and was to become one of the greatest names in Scottish journalism of the 20th century. One of his first moves was to appoint an Edinburgh man, William Veitch, as the Journal's London bureau chief.

Also in 1910, the company bought the neighbouring premises at 24 Broad Street for expansion. Shortly after, they bought an adjoining bakery and used that to create a purpose-built wire room for a much-improved telegraphy service between Broad Street and London.

By the outbreak of World War I, the Evening Express was selling 45,500 per day, compared to the Journal's 29,760. The directors steeled themselves for the upheaval which affects all newspapers when their country is at war.

The process is curiously predictable, as it has been throughout the history of newspapers. First, the labour supply diminishes, material costs rise and advertising revenue falls. This is balanced almost exactly by increased revenue from circulation as readers hunger for news from battle fronts. Broad Street witnessed a textbook example.

THE late autumn of 1917 was unseasonably warm in North Scotland. An early hairst led to a September and October so balmy and seductive that the horrors of war on the Continent seemed scarcely conceivable.

In Aberdeen, those citizens not occupied directly with the war or the war effort had taken to the streets to enjoy what remained of this Indian summer. Among them strolling on Union Street was a former pupil of Inverurie Academy, shortly to celebrate his 22nd birthday; the pride of graduating MA from Aberdeen University still fresh about him.

George Fraser was daydreaming as he walked; lost in thoughts of acquaintances and friends fighting in the trenches, and of the career crossroads at which he now stood when he was stopped by a friendly shout. Before him, beaming, stood a fellow-graduate, Alex Keith, from Kintore, who shook his hand warmly.

'George, what are you doing these days?'

'Not much. I've graduated, but now I don't know what I'm going to do. I was thinking I might go into teaching.'

'Och, never mind the teaching. I'm doing something much more interesting. I'm at the Journal. I've been there nine months. Never a dull moment. You'd like it yourself, I'm sure.'

'You think so? I've never given it a thought before.'

'Definitely. Listen, I'll have a word with them if you like and put your name up.'

George shrugged his shoulders. Within a fortnight, the aspiring teacher was the newest recruit at the offices of the Daily Journal and George Fraser had begun a career that was to last through nine decades and make him, eventually, Britain's oldest working journalist, author of the most durable column certainly in

ABOVE
Huntly Square in 1905. At the beginning of the 20th century, Huntly people were avid buyers of the Journal. At the century's end, little had changed. Press and Journal penetration at Huntly is among the paper's highest throughout its circulation area.

RIGHT
Broad Street, Aberdeen, at the beginning of the 20th century. Already this corner of the city centre had become the core of daily-paper journalism in the northern half of Scotland.

British journalism, and probably the world's.

Beginning in the dying days of World War I — on April 4, 1918, to be precise — his weekly thoughts were still appearing almost 80 years later as the 20th century drew to its close.

'I was recruited formally by one of the greatest names of Scottish Victorian journalism,' said George shortly before his 102nd birthday. 'He was William Maxwell. It was a very brief meeting. He explained what the job would entail and what I would be expected to do, and then he said: "By the way, journalists live to a ripe old age, you know." It was the only true thing the blighter told me.'

George was completely out of his depth when he started. He confesses now that he had not a single idea about journalism and was relieved when he was put to subbing [editing the work of reporters for grammar, spelling, punctuation and length, then composing appropriate headlines] the country news. He was put to country news, he said, probably because he came from the country, rather than because he had shown any aptitude.

'The tools of my trade were very simple: I had a black pencil for deletion, a pair of scissors for cutting up stories and a pot of paste and a brush for assembling the story on office paper so that it could be sent through to the compositors, or the comps, as we knew them.

'I say I was out of my depth, but journalism at that time was an immensely difficult job, anyway. In my defence, the fact that we were at war bore a deal of the responsibility for that.

'We were under censorship. Every single story — even the local stories that looked innocuous — had to be submitted to Dora. Dora was the thorn in our flesh: the Defence Of the Realm Act. Official censors were very strict about absolutely everything and erred on the side of caution. We couldn't even print the weather forecast.

'We were so limited by official censorship in so many, many ways that I look back now and wonder how we put out a newspaper at all. We were forced to hold back so much.

'All our foreign news came from the wire services and that had been screened before it reached us. It came on what we called flimsy; paper so thin that you could see daylight through it. It was virtually tissue paper. If you used too much gum when you were pasting up, the pencil just went straight through it.'

George started on 25/- (£1.25) a week for his first six months, and 15/- (75p) a week of that went on digs. After six months, his wage

The Journal's first delivery fleet — three hand-built wooden carts from an Aberdeen joiner

rose to 30/- (£1.50). A year later, he was salaried at £120 a year. To a young man in 1919, it was a fortune. As a lad of some means now, George felt able to start courting and set his cap at Peggy, a pretty young assistant to the Daily Journal cashier.

But George found he had a rival for Peggy's hand: a young reporter from the Mearns by the name of Leslie Mitchell. Mitchell asked Peggy to accompany him to the Tivoli Theatre to see a performance of Pygmalion. Peggy, by now smitten by George, replied that she was otherwise engaged. 'Ah, but had we been in Russia,' said Leslie, 'you would not have refused me.' He retreated to his desk.

'He was like that,' said George 80 years later. 'A bit of the bolshie persuasion. A nice chap, but bolshie. I think his trouble was that his folk wanted him to take over the farm, but he wanted to write.'

One evening, while he was late-duty reporter, Leslie Mitchell composed a love poem to Peggy and left it on her cashier's desk in the early hours of the morning. She kept it, but did not speak to her admirer about it.

Now, almost 80 years later, George still has the poem. Frequently, publishers, museum curators and students of Scottish literature approach him about it because Leslie Mitchell remains by far the most famous Daily Journal old boy.

Leslie Mitchell was Lewis Grassic Gibbon.

In any case, George and Peggy's courtship had to be put on hold for two years after George happened to meet a wounded soldier recuperating at Woodend General Hospital in the city. The soldier had been a Liverpool journalist and knew that his old paper, starved of talent, was looking for likely young recruits. The soldier sent a message to his old editor and, days later, George was offered £300 a year to move to Liverpool.

'It wasn't that I particularly wanted to leave the North-east,' he said, 'but I needed the money. In any case, it's always good to work on another paper.'

In 1921, he returned to see Peggy and his family when the River Don flooded near Kintore.

'For old times' sake, I wrote a story about the flood and sent it into the Journal,' he said. 'It appeared the next day on the leader page and I had a telegram from Maxwell asking me to come and see him.

' "Looking for chief sub [journalist in charge of a paper's sub-editors]," it said. "Offer £500 a year."

'I accepted.'

GEORGE returned to a company which, if not in trouble, was not performing particularly well. The circulation of the Journal was languishing between 15,000 and 20,000 and the paper was being carried by the Evening Express, which was outselling it five to one.

'Nowadays, a circulation of 15,000 for a morning paper seems incredibly small,' said George. 'But you must remember the circulation difficulties that papers faced in the northern half of Scotland.

'Our company had no vans. We relied on trains, postal subscriptions and casual sales. The postals made up the bulk of it. We often said out in the Garioch that some households ordered a Daily Journal just to be sure of getting the postie to call, because the posties were a bit more haphazard with their deliveries in those days.

'Unfortunately for us, many of the papers that were sent to country addresses did the rounds of seven or eight farms or houses over the course of a week because newspapers were still something of a luxury to country families on limited incomes. That all conspired to keep our circulation down.'

The parent company remained locally owned and had a board made up entirely of people from Aberdeen and the North-east. James Coutts, the general manager, held many of the shares and had developed the habit of paying the staff in shares, rather than money, which might have been taken as a mark of company health.

Not only was the company struggling to break even, its premises were growing daily more dilapidated. After only 27 years at Broad Street, the building's shortcomings were clear. Staff worked at space wherever they found it, frequently elbowing each other out of the way.

There was neither room nor money for expansion or redevelopment to cure the difficulties of housing a newspaper's many different disciplines in an efficient way.

Worse, while the Journal continued to flounder, the rival Free Press gave the impression of going from strength to strength commercially and journalistically, all of which undermined the mood in Broad Street.

Not only did the Free Press look brighter and more in tune with the times, it had the distinct advantage of more-modern premises, just round the corner on Union Street (now the Esslemont and Macintosh ladieswear building).

'I recall that our board looked at taking over the Athenaeum building, opposite the Town House for a while,' said George, 'but that came to nothing. So we just carried on as best we could.

'I wouldn't say there was great rivalry between the staffs on the two papers, but there was certainly a rivalry between the managements. At our level, we socialised well enough, but the two boards were highly competitive. You would have expected that.

'The only time I recall the truce being called was when the Free Press building went up in flames in 1919 and the Journal board approached the Press and offered to print their paper for them. It has always been a tradition in newspapers that even sworn rivals will help each other in times of distress.

'I still smile because I remember that one of our comps inserted a bogus advertisement in the Free Press pages that he was making up. Basically, he said that if Free Press readers wanted the best agricultural reporting, they should buy the Daily Journal.

'I don't know what the Free Press thought of it, but I can imagine. And I know that Maxwell thought the whole thing was hilarious.

'Now that I look back, the Journal and the Free Press must have been going through the same difficulties, although I suppose each staff thought the

FREE PRESS

ABOVE
The introduction of Linotype machines revolutionised the Daily Journal. Linotypes were still in use at Aberdeen Journals as recently as 1979.

LEFT
One of the few surviving pictures of the Aberdeen Free Press premises, now part of the Esslemont and Macintosh store in Union Street.

grass was greener on the other side. I always felt the Free Press had the better-educated journalists. It had a higher proportion of graduates. One of its editors had been Dr William Alexander, the man who wrote Johnny Gibb of Gushetneuk, which is still a classic of North-east literature.

'But the hard commercial fact was that the two papers were selling in much the same numbers to much the same area covering much the same news and were much the same size. The only difference was that the Journal was more inclined to the Tory view, while the Free Press was more Liberal.'

George's view is borne out by the figures. Neither paper was making money. The Journal was tired and rooted in the past, and the public knew it. The Free Press had suffered for its support of the Liberals when Liberal fortunes slumped after World War I. Each paper was draining its parent company's strength and both boards considered closing down their morning papers and concentrating efforts on their evenings.

The avenue was not explored for long. It became clear to both boards that the only sensible option was not co-ordinated closure of their mornings but something far bolder: amalgamation of the two companies. The approach was instigated by one of the Free Press proprietors, through a third party.

The fact that, more or less, the Free Press sought the amalgamation allowed William Maxwell, of the Journal, to be rather more bluff and bullish about it than his company's poor financial and circulation performance allowed, strictly speaking.

He wrote later, somewhat pompously: 'On our part, we would have bought them up, but their idea of the value of their property was absurd and there were other stipulations which our directors could not entertain.'

Behind the bluster lay hard and even-handed negotiation, culminating in an Extraordinary Meeting of Journal shareholders on November 3, 1922, when the board presented an Agreement for Amalgamation. The Free Press board held a similar meeting.

Both companies were to be liquidated and their assets pooled in a new company, Aberdeen Newspapers Ltd. The Evening Gazette would disappear and the

ABOVE
Either a blatantly posed picture or a very slow news day at the Daily Journal to have so many reporters at one time in the Literary Room (as the Editorial Department was known at the time).

RIGHT
Low Street, Banff, in the 1920s presents the affluent, genteel face of an elegant county town.

Evening Express would continue. The Free Press and the Daily Journal would combine titles to become the Aberdeen Press and Journal. All members of the Journal board would sit on the board of the new company, joined by only four members from the Free Press. William Maxwell, of the Journal, would become editor-in-chief of all the newspapers.

In a bizarre twist, Maxwell insisted that Broad Street would be the base for the new company, despite the fact that he knew perfectly well that the Free Press building on Union Street was immeasurably better. He confided later that he could not possibly have permitted closure of the Broad Street building, for that would have given the city the impression that the Free Press was taking over the Journal when, as everyone should surely know, the reverse was true.

The reverse was certainly not true, and quite why the amalgamation bargain that was struck was considered acceptable to the Free Press board is impossible to fathom at 75 years' remove. From being a company whose products were as healthy as its rival's, with brighter sales prospects, a marginally healthier advertising base and immeasurably superior premises, the Free Press lost its titles, its building and assumed a minority role in the new concern. William Maxwell pronounced himself satisfied with negotiations and the manner in which the amalgamation had been conducted. Not much wonder.

Amalgamating the companies posed relatively few problems compared to the immense difficulties of accommodating a four-newspaper quart in the dilapidated pint pot that was Broad Street.

There are no company records to show which staff members were retained, which were dismissed and on what basis but, as far as George Fraser recalls, it was all carried out quickly, sensitively and amicably.

'There was great anxiety on both staffs as to who would get what jobs,' he said, 'but as far as I remember there was no great fuss at the end of the day. It just made things even tighter at Broad Street. We knocked through into another building or two along the street and expanded that way, but we discovered that none of the neighbouring buildings' floors was on the same level, so when the builders knocked through from one into the other, we had to create steps up or steps down so the floors would meet. It made the whole place even more of a rabbit warren.

'The hardest thing to swallow, to be perfectly honest, was the title of the amalgamated morning papers. I can remember we all sat thinking how ugly and clumsy it was.

' "Aberdeen Press and Journal".

'It hardly tripped off the tongue. We were all certain that it wouldn't last. It couldn't possibly. We were sure that it would have to be changed within months to a name that sounded a bit more sensible. Whoever had heard of a newspaper being called something like Aberdeen Press and Journal, after all?'

As for the readers, they seemed to accept it remarkably easily. Apart from the change of title, they might have noticed most the change in politics. Maxwell had stipulated that the new Aberdeen Press and Journal was to be absolutely even-handed politically. There was to be no

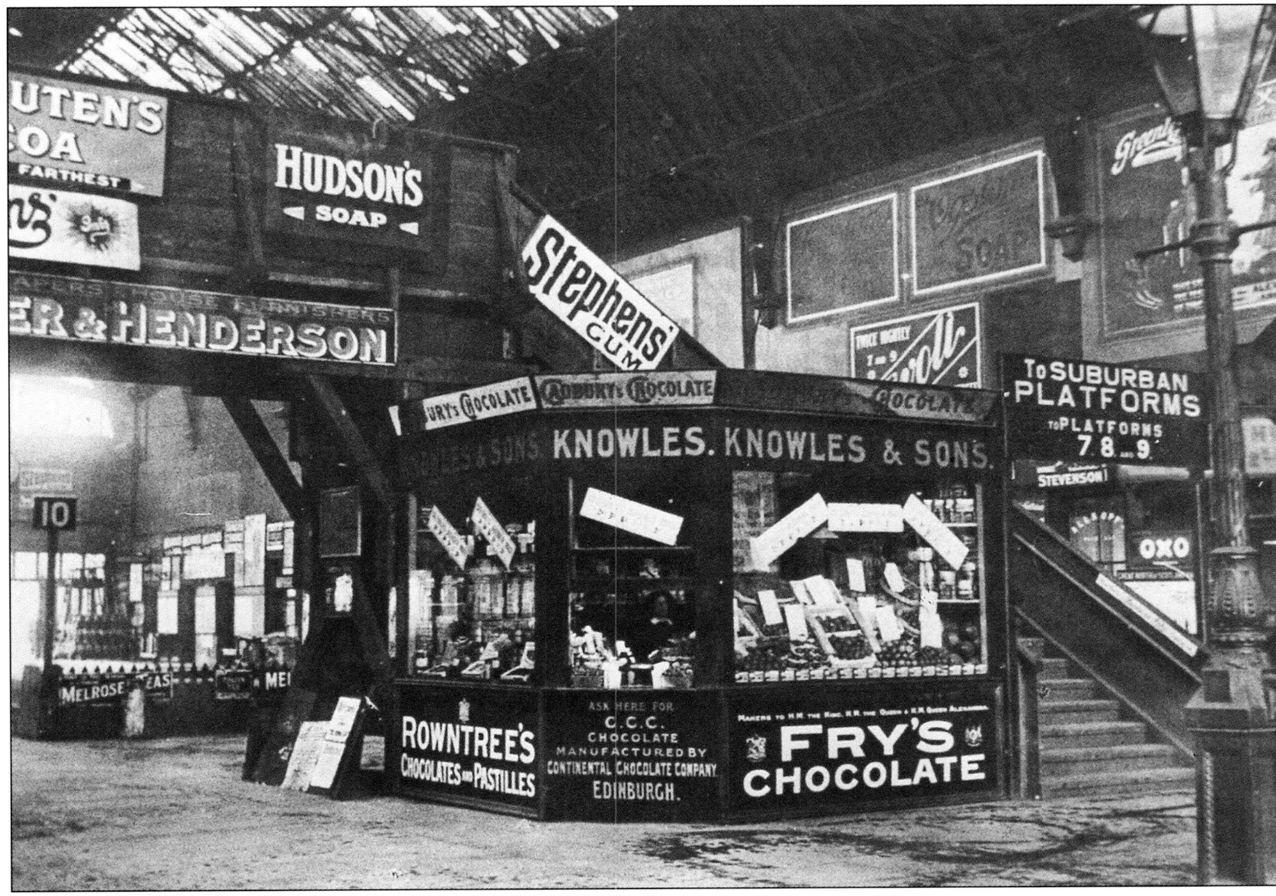

ABERDEEN 'subbie' station in 1920. Lines to Deeside and Buchan ran from here, and Daily Journals and Free Presses were dispatched through here six mornings a week.

The tradition was maintained by their successor, the Aberdeen Press and Journal.

M'HARDY,
rchants.

Aberdeen Daily Journal.

THURSDAY, NOVEMBER 30, 1922.

THREE HALFPENCE.

PUBLIC NOTICES.

SALE OF ANTIQUE PERSIAN RUGS.

SUPERB COLLECTION OF ABOVE RUGS

WILL BE SHOWN BY

Mr A. GALLINDORS,

At the PALACE HOTEL, Aberdeen,
From 30th Nov. till 10th Dec., 1922.

ABERDEEN HARBOUR.

PROPERTIES FOR SALE

SITUATIONS VACANT.

AMUSEMENTS.

W. W. KELLY'S Powerful Company

"A ROYAL DIVORCE."

THE BAND OF THE BRITISH LEGION

"THE BATTLE OF WATERLOO."

The Lyric Amateur Opera Company

"MERRIE ENGLAND."

THE FURNISHING HOUSE FO

GALLOWAY & SYKES, A

PIANO REPAIRS.

Haigh
Hou

M'Hardy
ERCHANTS.

The Aberdeen Free Press.

No. 16,823. ABERDEEN, THURSDAY, NOVEMBER 30, 1922. Price, Three-Halfpence.

SETTEES &
for COM
JOHN ALEXAN
257 UNION
ABERD

Scottish Orchestra

Entertainments.

HIS MAJESTY'S THEATRE.

W. W. KELLY'S Powerful Company

"A ROYAL DIVORCE."

THE BAND OF THE BRITISH LEGION

"THE BATTLE OF WATERLOO."

The Lyric Amateur Opera Company

"MERRIE ENGLAND."

Situations Vacant.

Agricultural & Live Stock Sales.

Auction Sales.

McDOUGALL & S

LIMITED

CHINA MERCHANTS

Great STOCK-REDUCING

4/- IN THE £.

CASH DURING SALE.

McDOUGALL & SONS.

500 UNION STREET.

partisanship or favour. It was a policy that ruffled feathers in both political camps.

'And he stuck to it,' said George. 'We had the usual nonsense that all journalists get of politicians from one side complaining that they got a half-inch less coverage on some such issue on whatever day than their opponents, but he just ignored that. I have vague memories of him being visited by councillors or politicians trying to persuade the paper's policy to their view, but none of them succeeded.'

For some weeks, the circulation, advertising and editorial results of the amalgamation were monitored closely. By the middle of 1923, it became clear that the gamble had worked. The new company was returning steady, if not particularly spectacular, profits. Its papers were building circulation slowly.

In 1924, the company put the Free Press building on the market at £25,000 and found an eager buyer in an expansion-minded Esslemont and Macintosh department store. In 1925, William Maxwell was appointed to the board of the company.

At Easter 1927, however, Maxwell stumbled and fell while stepping from a bus outside the Palace Hotel in Union Street. He contracted phlebitis, a condition so grave that the board could not

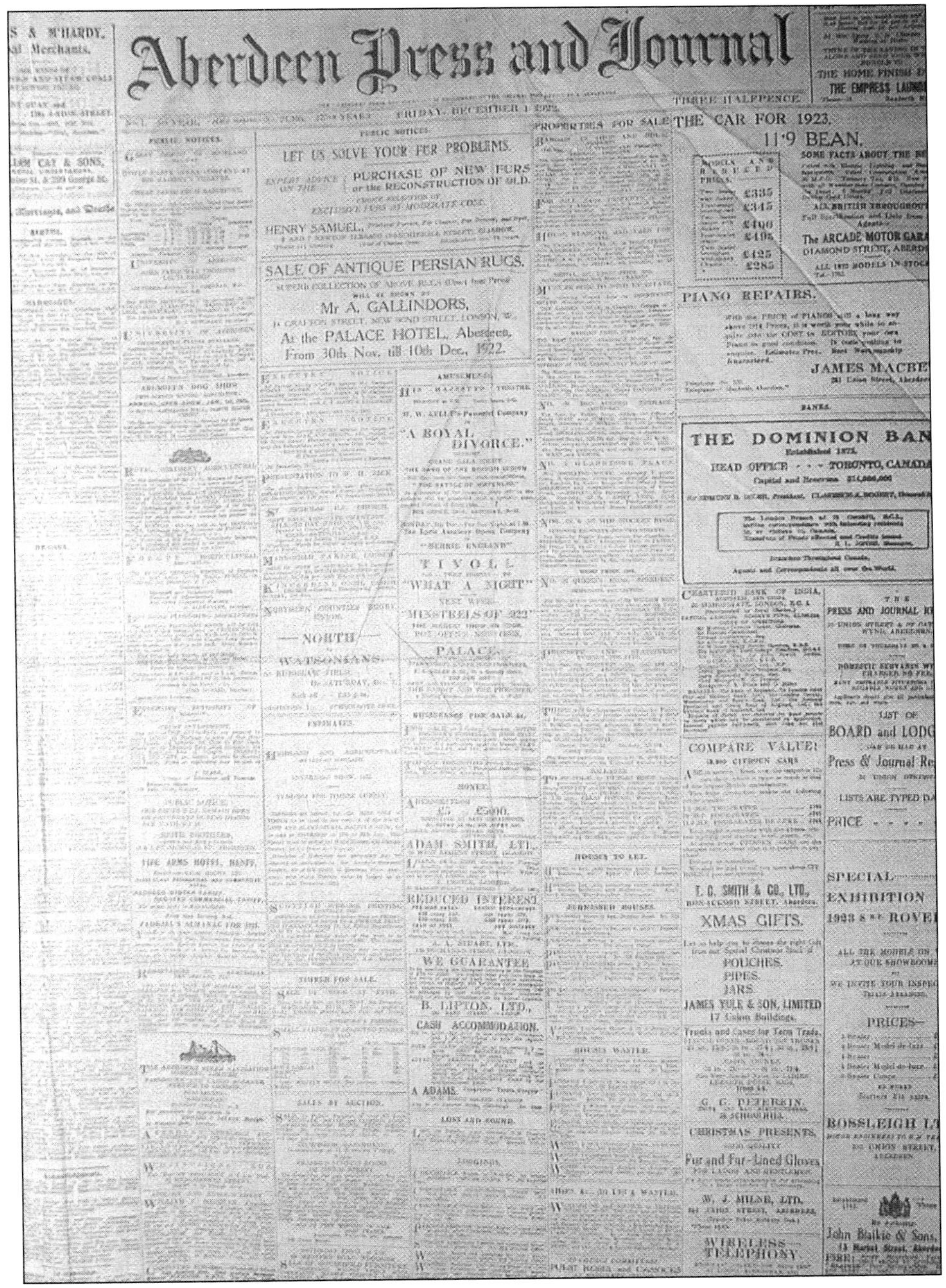

Aberdeen Press and Journal

THREE HALFPENCE

FRIDAY, DECEMBER 1, 1922.

THE CAR FOR 1923.

11·9 BEAN.

LET US SOLVE YOUR FUR PROBLEMS.

PURCHASE OF NEW FURS or the RECONSTRUCTION OF OLD.

HENRY SAMUEL,

SALE OF ANTIQUE PERSIAN RUGS.

Mr A. GALLINDORS,

At the PALACE HOTEL, Aberdeen, From 30th Nov. till 10th Dec., 1922.

PIANO REPAIRS.

"A ROYAL DIVORCE."

TIVOLI.

"WHAT A NIGHT"

MINSTRELS OF 1922

NORTH

WATSONIANS.

PALACE.

COMPARE VALUE!

ADAM SMITH, LTD.

REDUCED INTEREST

WE GUARANTEE

B. LIPTON, LTD.

CASH ACCOMMODATION.

A. ADAMS.

T. C. SMITH & CO., LTD.

XMAS GIFTS.

POUCHES.

PIPES.

JARS.

JAMES YULE & SON, LIMITED

G. G. PETERKIN.

CHRISTMAS PRESENTS.

Fur and Fur-Lined Gloves

W. J. MILNE, LTD.

WIRELESS TELEPHONY.

SPECIAL EXHIBITION

BOSSLEIGH

John Blaikie & Sons,

LEFT

On November 30, 1922, the Aberdeen Daily Journal (top) and the Aberdeen Free Press (bottom) published their last editions before joining forces. The next morning saw a new masthead appear for the first time.

RIGHT

On December 1, 1922, came North Scotland's first encounter with the name Press and Journal.

FORSYTH HOTEL
20
6A
CASTLE ST
TRAMWAY
STATION
77
CORPORATION

CHAPTER IV

P&J Goes to War

BROAD STREET employees were naturally wary before and immediately after the takeover by the Berry Brothers and the Allied Newspapers Group. New owners unsettle any workforce.

The guardedness did not last for long. It became clear quickly that Allied intended not to milk Aberdeen for easy profit, but were determined to invest heavily and to develop their new papers.

By the beginning of 1929, the security of being part of one of the world's biggest newspaper groups became clear. The Aberdeen Press and Journal now had direct access to a custom service of international wire reports (organised by Ian Fleming, later to find fame as James Bond's creator).

There was also fuller coverage of national news, in a volume and breadth which the London bureau of old could not have matched. Conferences involving all regional newspapers in the Allied Group promoted the exchange of ideas and experimental journalism. The Berrys founded a group training scheme for new journalists. Professionally, all employees found that promotion prospects multiplied suddenly beyond expectation, given the overnight inheritance of so many sister newspapers throughout the Commonwealth.

The Berrys insisted that trades unions be established formally, because they preferred to negotiate through recognised unions, rather than individually. They insisted, too, that every employee be offered the chance to join. Most didn't.

Best of all for many, the Berrys increased almost all wages and salaries, bringing them into line with others in the Allied Group. With that final flourish, the Berrys ensured that few Aberdeen employees could sustain their practised chariness, disgruntlement and cynicism for long. In many ways, the Berry ownership was a golden age for newspaper employees in Aberdeen. Rarely have a

Enamel advertising placards such as these were familiar throughout the North and North-east between the wars.

Today, collectors snap them up at memorabilia auctions.

Traffic jams in Union Street, Aberdeen, were as frustrating in years gone by as they are now.

newspaper company's management and staff been pulling so sincerely and effectively in same direction.

Not every Scot welcomed the Berry Brothers' ownership of the Aberdeen papers. A leading article in the Edinburgh Evening Dispatch declaimed:

'It must be regretted by all who are solicitous for what is best in Scottish life that Aberdeen has gone over to the enemy. The independence of the Scottish Press is being rapidly eroded, a development that will subtly and adversely react upon the whole national life. Every true Scot must regret the capitulation of the granite citadel of the North, which furnishes yet another milestone in the onward march of Anglification.'

In news terms, the Thirties were something of a mixed bag. They were strong nationally, with the Depression, the Abdication crisis, the R101 airship crash and the novelty of the first Royal Christmas broadcast. The international diet was healthy, too: Amy Johnson flew solo to Australia, Edison died, Jesse Owens won his gold medals at the Berlin Olympics and, most ominously, Hitler became German chancellor.

In terms of local news, the Thirties were notoriously lean — apart from one tale which had the country riveted, and which many older Aberdonians recall even now.

Dawn was just breaking on Saturday, April 21, 1934, when the body of eight-year-old Helen Priestly was discovered tied up in a sack in the lobby of the tenement at 61 Urquhart Road. She had been missing since Friday lunchtime, when her mother had sent her to buy a loaf. By 7pm, a search party had been organised. At midnight, they had found nothing and decided to meet again at first light.

The sack was discovered almost at once the following morning. Helen had suffered the most appalling sexual assault: one of the most violent rapes Scottish police had known. She appeared to have been strangled, too. The sack yielded several clues, but police suspected that someone in the search party had been the killer, for the sack could not possibly have been overlooked the night before.

Four days later, in the sma oors of Thursday morning, police arrived at 61 Urquhart Road and went straight to the flat above the Priestlys. They arrested Alexander and Jeannie Donald, both 38. Even at that time in the morning, a crowd gathered to jeer and howl abuse. More remarkable still, in the minutes that it took the Black Maria to travel down King Street to Lodge Walk, a crowd put at 2,000 had gathered outside police HQ and their mood was foul and vengeful.

Husband and wife were charged with assault by seizing their victim, holding her, compressing her throat, cutting or stabbing her, and murdering her. Two days later, the police pathologist announced that he had established that Alexander Donald had been at work at the time of Helen's death and could not possibly have been involved. He was freed, and Jeannie Donald was left to face the charge alone.

At Edinburgh High Court 10 weeks later, Jeannie Donald pleaded not guilty. Throughout her trial, she sat motionless and

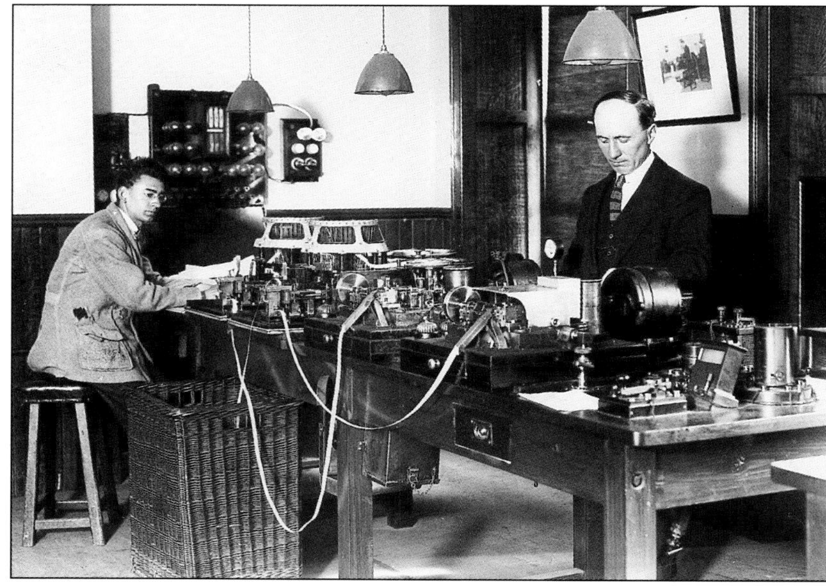

ABOVE
The Wire Room, Broad Street, brought news from agencies and correspondents around Britain and throughout the world and was regarded as the height of technology in its day. This picture was taken 1929, shortly after the Berry brothers took over and began a campaign of heavy investment.

RIGHT
Dispatch in the early 1930s was not the smooth, computerised affair that it is now.

Press and

The size of the press between the wars and the number of men required to operate it pales beside the two post-war giants which were several times this size, and the hi-tech Goss Colorliner of the end of the century.

expressionless. Her own daughter testified that Jeannie had had an unusual French loaf in her kitchen on the evening of Helen's disappearance. It turned out to have been the loaf Helen's mother had asked Helen to buy from the nearby shop.

Forensic evidence was even more damning. Bacteria on Jeannie Donald's dishcloth matched bacteria on the dead girl's clothes. The only defence left to Jeannie Donald was the violent rape — surely a sign of a male murderer.

In fact, the rape was artificial; probably inflicted by a broom handle in the panic after the murder. That a woman should commit such a violent assault on a small girl only compounded the jury's horror. It took them just 18 minutes to find Jeannie Donald guilty. She was sentenced to hang, but the death penalty was commuted to life imprisonment. She was released in 1944.

Two mysteries remain. First, what was the motive? The most common theory at the time was that the motive was horribly thin: the wee girl had been playing pranks on the downstairs neighbour, whom she did not like. Jeannie Donald had lost her temper and, in her rage, had gone too far.

Second, what led the police to the Donalds' flat so unexpectedly? That has never been understood properly — until now.

George Fraser recalled clearly that Herbert Catto, son of the Evening Express editor, had an obsessive interest in the case and, while the police conducted their painstaking interviews, Herbert had spent several evenings nosing around the Urquhart Road, Urquhart Street, King Street area talking to people and soaking up the atmosphere.

'It struck him that something was odd about the Priestlys' tenement,' said George. 'Then he realised that while every other tenement for streets around had lights in the window, the ground-floor flat at number 61 never did. The Donalds were lying low, and the fact that they were not behaving normally made Herbert suspicious. He mentioned it to a senior police officer on the case. Arrests followed within hours. I cite that as a classic example of newspapers doing their bit for law and order.

'Our reward was seeing the case concluded although, I might add, the papers' circulations broke 100,000 during the story's run.'

Herbert Catto's reward was accelerated progress through the journalistic ranks. Within 10 years, he was chief reporter and is still remembered as one of the finest and most resourceful reporters the Journals produced.

IN 1937, THE older of the two Berry brothers, William, left Allied Newspapers to develop other interests, leaving the group in sole control of brother Gomer, soon to be Lord Kemsley.

When war clouds began gathering over Europe in 1938, Allied commissioned staff and freelance journalists to travel round the Continent gauging tensions in key cities and countries. Those pre-war dispatches appeared weekly in the Aberdeen papers, ensuring that readers in North Scotland were as well informed as readers in the Home Counties.

But foreseeing the inevitable did not make its arrival any easier to bear. For the second time in 25 years, the Press and Journal (Aberdeen was dropped from its title in May, 1939) and Evening Express steeled themselves for the well-known War Effect on newspaper operations. Almost at once, the young men of the staff were called up and left for battle training. Their elders raised a unit of the Home Guard and established a fire-watch rota.

Papers became smaller as newsprint supplies diminished and costs increased. Even ink was at a premium. The company convened a committee to plan for bomb damage. On the assumption that the Luftwaffe might find Aberdeen a tempting target, bomb damage seemed inevitable and the presses had to be protected. The only solution was to dismantle and rebuild them in the basement.

It was all familiar territory for George Fraser. 'Dora returned with a vengeance,' he said. 'The Defence of the Realm Act and the censors were as active in the second war as they had been in the first. I remember one ridiculous occasion when a German bomber flew over Broad Street, so low that I felt I could almost reach out and touch him, and went on to hit Hall Russell's shipyard.

'We couldn't get the story in the

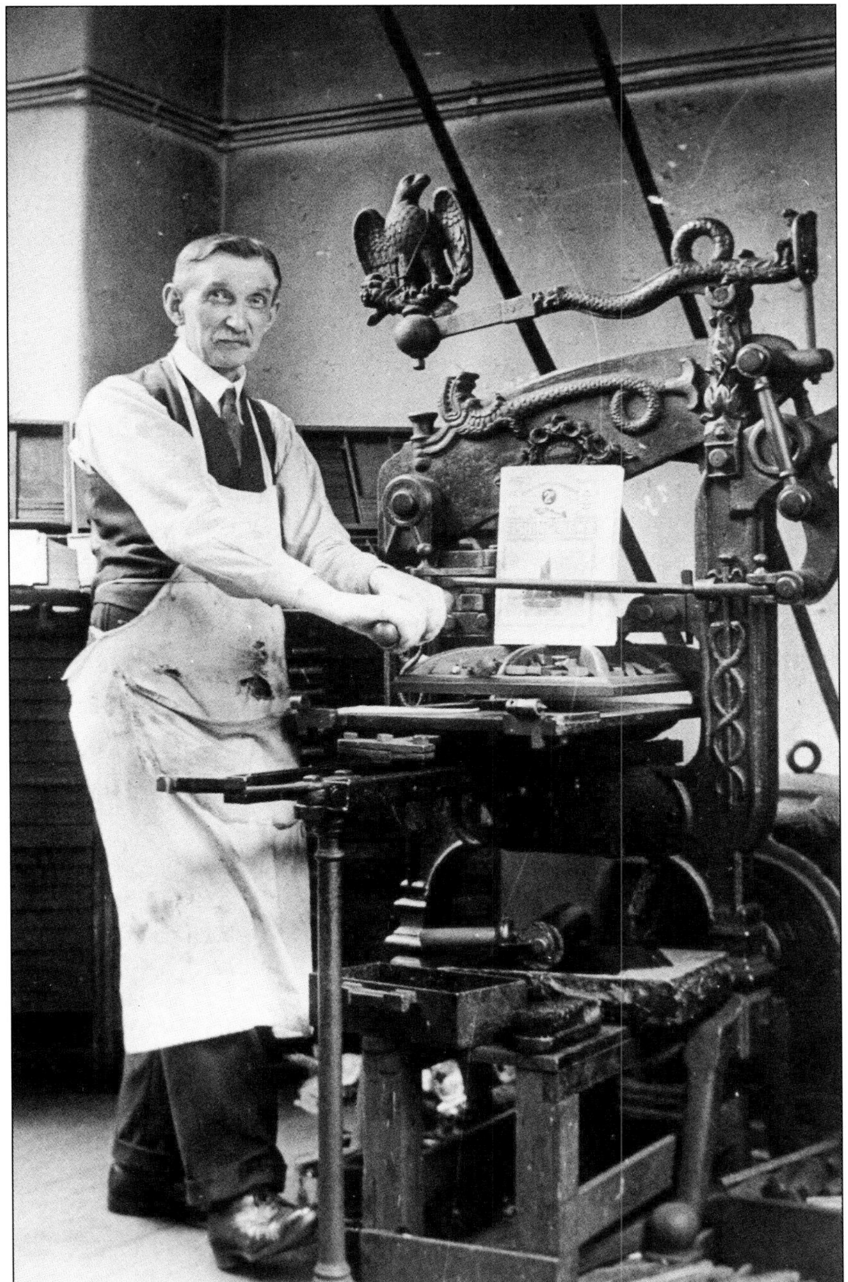

The Eagle hand press which printed news of the Battle of Waterloo was still in use 120 years later, turning out another Aberdeen Journals publication, the Fishing News

paper thanks to Dora. It seemed ridiculous to us at the time, and it seems just as ridiculous now. Everybody in the city knew what had happened, but we couldn't tell them as much.

'My other striking memory was of the staffing we had. The numbers were reduced of course, but the staff was very, very young or very, very old. Just about every company at the time could have said the same, I suppose.

'We also had a few poor chaps who had been invalided out of the Services because they were battle-shocked.

'Sometimes the whole pressure of newspapers would just become too much for them and they would begin reading stories aloud to themselves in the most pitiful, anguished voices, but there was nothing we could do to comfort them. Pitiful.'

Broad Street's anti-bomb measures were never tested in anger.

Not once was production disrupted by enemy activity, although newsprint shortages and ink shortages bit ever deeper as the war progressed.

Eventually, the Evening Express decided to tackle the newsprint shortage by converting to tabloid size for the duration, a decision that was not reversed until 1958. Company records show vehement complaints from the public about the conversion to tabloid and, newspaper readers being newspaper readers, the same vehement complaints when the paper switched back to broadsheet size.

But if war constrained journalism, it also laid the ground for several unexpected and distinguished careers. Notably, it gave women ready access to a career which had been almost exclusively male.

At Broad Street HQ, the Registry was a small room off the advertising department which specialised in processing advertisements for housemaids, nannies and kitchie deems. Demand for domestics withered with the war so Kathleen Findlay, who was in charge of the Registry, was asked to fill her day by taking on typing for the Press and Journal news editor, a Banffshire man, James M. Chalmers (no relation to the founding family).

When Miss Findlay left to marry, her deputy was brought in

Among the most frequent advertisers in Aberdeen Journals publications between the wars were the Isaac Benzie drapery stores. Most customers remember the huge store in George Street, Aberdeen, (renamed Arnotts in 1973), but this was a branch at 73 Victoria Road, Torry. It closed in 1934.

as a replacement. The deputy's name was Ethel Simpson.

'Mr Chalmers was always Mr Chalmers to me, and I was always Miss Simpson to him,' said Ethel. 'He was gey oldey-worldy when it came to women on his staff, but he was also one of the most courteous people I have known. I ran his messages for months until he trusted me with minor journalistic tasks, probably because there was no one else to do them.

'I was the one who would file cuttings and pictures in the library. I answered the phone. I picked up dispatches at the Joint Station from the correspondents. I went out to collect pictures of war casualties from their families. It wasn't until six weeks before D Day that he told me I was going to be made a reporter.'

While Ethel's long-coveted big break had landed in her lap, big changes were taking place at the other end of the hierarchy, too. At much the same time, the Aberdeen board decided that expecting William Veitch to act as Editor across its entire stable of papers was to ask too much of one man, especially with the extraordinary demands of wartime.

Mr Veitch was offered promotion to the figurehead role of Editor-in-Chief of all publications. He accepted.

ABOVE
Sub-editing the Press and Journal during a power cut. On the extreme left is a very young Jimmy Grant, later to become one of the great names of the Press and Journal.

LEFT
Within weeks of this picture being taken in 1941, the majestic Palace Hotel in Union Street, Aberdeen, was a burned-out shell.

George Fraser was asked to become editor of the Evening Express, while James M. Chalmers was appointed Editor of the Press and Journal.

Later, Cuthbert Graham became editor of an often overlooked Broad Street publication. The Weekly Journal was the most direct descendant of the original Aberdeen's Journal. When the Journal had begun daily publication in 1872, the old weekly paper had been maintained, shifted from hard news to a more featurey tone and renamed.

The new executives had little time to find their feet, but the transitions appear to have been smooth. Ethel, meanwhile, was preparing excitedly for her first day as a full-time professional journalist. She turned up for work to be teamed with a young reporter of the same age, although much more seasoned in the ways of journalism, Gordon Forbes. Mr Chalmers instructed Gordon to take good care of the newest recruit and to 'see that nothing offensive should befall her'.

'I still remember my first outing with Gordon,' said Ethel, 'because before we left for the Police Court, Mr Chalmers took me to his office and explained that if any nasty cases came up, I should leave the room. I obeyed him, because I had been brought

LEFT
The Press and Journal in wartime was filled with heartbreaking pictures such as this Peterhead child being cradled gently from the aftermath of a bombing raid on the town.

RIGHT
Sales of the papers began to pick up as Allied fortunes began to improve. Crowds such as these gladdened the heart of any circulation manager.

up to do what I was tell't, but I was so desperate to be a real reporter that I stood outside with my lug pressed against the door. When I went back in, Jock Adams, a great character of a town sergeant, would stand beside me at the Press bench and, out of the side of his mouth, would tell me all the details. It took me a lang time, being as green as a cabbage, to get the grip of lewd and libidinous practices.

'It's remarkable how all the traditional work of local news-gathering and reporting was kept going despite all the wartime difficulties.

'When it was very warm, we would have lemonade and sliders from Ledingham's shoppie across the road, and the Bond Bar was a home from home for the men. The City Bar became famous as the Press howff.'

George Rowntree Harvey acted as drama and music critic for the Journals and, as Ethel recalled, not always successfully. Once, in a crit of a Carl Rosa Opera Company production, he wrote:

'Ruth Naylor wore a wig which suited neither her face nor the part she was playing.'

Miss Naylor was furious, mostly because it was her own hair.

'By May, 1944, we were all getting hyped up for the start of the Second Front,' said Ethel.

'By the August, we were all beginning to talk about the end of the war. By April, 1945, the stories and pictures of Nazi concentration camps were beginning to come through, and they were just atrocious.

'On May 2, according to my diary, a flash came through on the wire that Hitler was dead. The last air-raid siren went and we all thought that the Nazis were making a last stand, then came a public announcement that we had just heard the siren for the last time.'

But there was heartache in the joy. Ethel was dispatched to a house in Prospect Terrace, supposedly to meet a soldier who had been repatriated after five years in a German PoW camp, only to find that the soldier's father had died suddenly the night before. The old man's joy in seeing his son alive had been too much for him.

On May 9, Ethel's diary noted: 'Victory at last', although, as she recalls now: 'The thrill for me was blighted by the confusion of information coming out in bits and pieces.

'A flash on the radio that night said that the Tuesday would be a public holiday to mark Victory in Europe. I didn't know whether to go into work, but I did. I was just about the only one on the train from Inverurie. The whole staff was on as usual. Flags were

24
EVENING EXPRESS

everywhere and we had two hanging from the reporters' windows. About three in the afternoon, a huge crowd gathered outside the Town House and all the ships' hooters in the Harbour began to blast and kirk bells were ringing all over the place.

'All the men in the company came to the reporters' room to hear Mr Churchill's victory speech, and George Ley Smith took it down in shorthand to rush it for the EE. He took me through to his room to type out his shorthand for him. I hadn't time to check a thing. It was being nipped out of my hands and shoved down the chute. That was exciting.

'Of course, I knew that the end of the war would bring changes. Mainly, all the old boys would be back from the war, and their jobs were guaranteed to them. I had more than a few worries that I wouldn't survive. My heart was definitely in reporting and I was determined to keep it there.'

She did.

WE WON'T leave World War II without recalling a key chapter in the Press and Journal's history.

In 1940, the men of the 51st (Highland) Division had made a last stand against advancing Nazi troops at St Valéry-en-Caux, a small town on the Normandy coast, a few miles west of Dieppe. Ultimately, the men surrendered, but not without great loss of life.

In defiance of the Nazis, the men, women and children of the town protected the Scots, cared for the wounded and paid homage to the dead.

Five years later, with hostilities past, the Press and Journal suggested that the North and North-east might like to show gratitude to the French town that had stood shoulder to shoulder with young Scots lads. The paper launched the St Valéry Remembrance Appeal. Every town and village throughout the circulation area contributed, raising £8,729.

Originally, the fund committee had wanted to do something to help the French people rebuild their shattered town. Instead, the townspeople asked for a memorial gateway to their military cemetery and a Salle d'Écosse in their new council chambers.

The committee agreed at once, and Kemnay-granite pillars and Aboyne-oak gates were carved and dispatched in time for an inaugural ceremony in France in June, 1950.

William Veitch represented the Press and Journal. Lady Huntly, daughter of Lord Kemsley, gave the inaugural address. Later that day, a Highland Division monument, also of Kemnay granite, was unveiled on the cliffs of St Valéry. It was a moving ceremony, attended by many of the ordinary folk of the northern half of Scotland, come to pay homage to fallen sons, brothers, fathers and sweethearts and to offer personal thanks to the people of one of the bravest little towns in France.

FAR LEFT
VE Day in Broad Street.

ABOVE
Lord Kemsley's portrait was paid for by Aberdeen Journals staff to mark the 200th birthday of the Press and Journal in 1948.

CHAPTER V

At Death's Door

THE euphoria of victory over Germany fizzled within weeks as the nation set about rebuilding after war and coming to terms with the uncomfortable truth that strictures and sacrifices born in conflict linger long after hostilities cease.

The Press and Journal found newsprint and ink every bit as hard to come by in the post-war years as they had been in the darkest depths of war. Papers remained thin for far longer than the board had dreamed. The Press and Journal of the late 1940s rarely exceeded 10 pages. More often, it amounted to only eight.

Aberdeen was not alone in this; throughout the country, every other newspaper publisher faced the same strictures. But the fact that newspapers nationwide were facing much the same difficulties of supply cut little ice with Press and Journal readers. Then, as now, they appreciated value for money and were inclined to turn against a paper which they felt was not playing a straight hand.

At least, that was how a board meeting in early 1946 explained a gentle and steady decline in circulation. It was an especially frustrating time for the Press and Journal; for once it was suffering because of difficulties entirely outwith its control.

The gloom dissipated briefly, but spectacularly, in January, 1948, when the Press and Journal reached its 200th birthday.

The celebrations came at precisely the right time, and not just for the paper and its staff. The public throughout northern Scotland had suffered post-war rationing for far longer than they had expected, and the excuse for a party — even someone else's party — was too good to let pass. Throughout the circulation area, Aberdeen Journals arranged receptions for community notables and long-standing readers, as well as sponsored concert evenings and free cinema shows.

But the biggest celebrations were in Aberdeen, attended by more than 1,000 invited guests. Civic dignitaries, business leaders,

A post-war December Monday washday at the old town quayside drying-green at Stonehaven.

Well-earned breather from the heat of the foundry

academics and clergy were treated to a bicentenary banquet at the Music Hall, while virtually every member of Aberdeen Journals staff packed the Music Hall for a bicentenary party.

Lord Kemsley footed both bills personally. Editor-in-chief Veitch read formal congratulations from King George VI, the prime ministers of Canada, Australia, New Zealand and South Africa, as well as from the oldest newspapers in the US, Australia, New Zealand, Norway and Sweden.

A writer of the time noted that 'history does not record that champagne flowed at the inauguration ceremony 200 years ago, but the bicentenary was well and truly toasted with well-filled glasses'.

Ethel Simpson puts it a little more robustly: 'Boy, the drink flowed. We'd never seen anything like it. Everything was free, and you can imagine how well that went down in 1948. Mr Veitch had to close the bar more than once at the staff do, but it just opened again.

'Many were the sore heads after our party.

'And it wasn't just at the staff function. It was the same story at the banquet for the great and the good at the Music Hall. Old Lady Aberdeen was at the toffs' do and she was found hanging on to a pillar.'

THE paper had a new Editor in 1950. James M. Chalmers moved to a post at London head office and was succeeded by George Ley Smith, an Aberdonian. George was noted for his athletic past, and for being at the centre of a 1920s story which passed into Scottish journalistic legend.

As a young reporter, he had been covering the stranding of a trawler off Balmedie, north of Aberdeen, in a violent storm late one night. Repeated attempts to fire a line aboard had come to nothing. Eventually, George had drawn the senior policeman aside to say that, as he had four international swimming caps to his credit, he was probably the best swimmer there and was

FAR LEFT
Festivities in full swing at the staff dance in 1948 to mark the bicentenary of the Press and Journal.

LEFT
George Ley Smith, champion swimmer, shy hero and ultimately Editor of the Press and Journal from 1950 to 1956.

RIGHT
Once the wire room had been decanted to the top floor of Broad Street in 1948, there was space to take advantage of the latest technology.

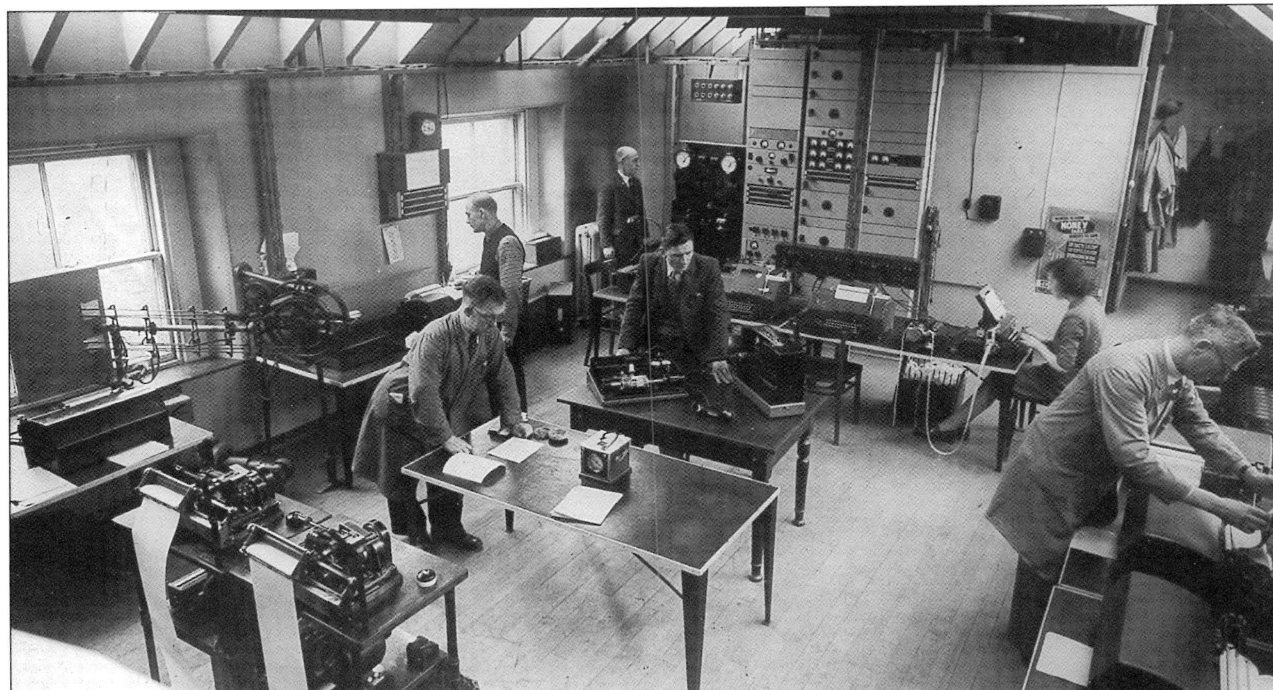

quite willing to strike out to the vessel with a line.

The senior officer had been dubious, but George had begun stripping off, had called for a line and had waded in. He had struggled for almost an hour against impossible odds. He had failed, but his bravery had been beyond question. He had returned to Broad Street a little later than he had hoped, but still in time for the edition. He had turned in crisp and clean copy and, as far as his colleagues were concerned, that had been that. George had not mentioned his rescue effort.

Next morning, the national papers had seized on the bravery of the courageous stranger. George's incredulous colleagues presented him with a gold watch a few days later.

APART from the Coronation, the most notable story during George's editorship was the infamous Great Gale of 1953. A balmy January ended with what still ranks as the most violent storm of 20th-century Scotland. Entire forests were flattened, ferries sank, houses were demolished, trains derailed, boats blown ashore and cars upended. The fishing hamlets of Pennan, Aberdeenshire, and Crovie, Banffshire, were damaged almost beyond repair in a few hours.

The scale of the devastation escaped the Government, which seemed to concentrate on the appalling flooding in Norfolk and Suffolk, unaware how badly North-east Scotland had borne the brunt, too.

Only when the House of Commons was shown the Press and Journal picture spreads of wholesale damage from coast to mountaintop did MPs set up a Scottish emergency committee.

FR38
BF 277

LEFT
The biggest regional story of the Fifties. Vast swathes of North-east Scotland were flattened by the Great Gale of January, 1953. This was Pennan.

BELOW
Wrapping subscription copies was a tiresome task. Almost 20,000 daily copies of the Press and Journal went by post in the 1950s and 1960s.

George Ley Smith's health began to fail shortly after, and he was replaced in 1956 by Evening Express Editor Ken Peters.

The following year, William Veitch retired as Editor-in-chief. He had been the dominant figure in Aberdeen newspapers for three decades, and many surviving journalists still recall the pervasive influence and patriarchy of WV, as he was known.

'His was the last word,' said Gordon Forbes, a sports reporter in WV's latter years. 'I remember that I was asked to transfer from the Evening Express to the Press and Journal in 1956. I wasn't too happy about that because I played a lot of sport in the evenings and, obviously, when you work on a morning paper you have to work evenings most of the time.

'I went to WV and said I wasn't very keen on moving and I hoped that it wasn't compulsory.

' "Not at all," he said. "It's not compulsory. You can always look for another job somewhere else."

'When WV was Editor-in-chief, the editors would get a copy of each day's paper from him with red circles on a lot of the pages. He would circle mis-spellings, bad grammar, facts which didn't tally and basic things which offended his sense of good journalism. He was pernickety, I'll say that for him.'

He certainly was. In 1952, in the Kemsley Manual of Journalism, a mighty hardback tome setting down the trade principles, WV contributed a chapter on standards of reporting, and concluded:

'Excusably but undeniably, the young and not-so-young reporter, whose cultural and technical development was interrupted by the war, is not fully trained. I might add that he is in danger of overlooking the clarity of simple English. A proneness to Americanised clichés, or perhaps cinematised jargon, does tend to obscure many young reporters' natural expression and elucidation.'

Yet for every journalist who found WV a forbidding, irascible character, there was one who found him avuncular and encouraging. Duncan MacRae, ultimately deputy editor and Highland Editor until his retirement in 1996, joined the paper in 1955 as a junior sub-editor and recalls WV as 'a small, bald mannie with a big desk, but always very amenable. I found him exceptionally pleasant to me. His guiding principle for his staff was that they had to earn standing in the community, be well-educated and properly dressed, and there's nothing wrong with that.'

Pearl Murray, a Strichen teenager with a burning ambition to be a journalist, left Fraserburgh Academy in the late 1940s and went promptly to Broad Street to see about a job.

'Mr Veitch was very kind to me,' she said. 'He listened to what I had to say and then said: "Look, go into local weekly newspapers. Learn your craft there by doing anything and everything. It'll be tough, but if you survive that, come back to me in a few years and I'll see what we might do."

'It was excellent advice. I went to the Turriff and Inverurie papers and learned the trade from the ground up. A few years later, I happened to be at the opening of a fashion shop and bumped into Mr Veitch by chance. He invited me for interview and he took me on. He gave me six months in every Editorial department at the Journals.

'It was a quite incredible arrangement; quite unprecedented. No one else had been given advanced training like that, and I'm still grateful.

'I wouldn't say he was a warm man. He was an extremely remote figure, but he was most certainly a man of his word.'

For all his gravitas and authority, Mr Veitch was not above being upbraided. Gordon Forbes recalls that Bob Boothby, then Tory MP for East Aberdeenshire, was a regular visitor to Broad Street in the 1950s, where he would warm himself at the fire, conversing loudly all the while in that peculiarly booming voice.

'One day, he and WV had turned up beside the subs, and Boothby was being really noisy, almost shouting his conversation. It wouldn't have mattered much usually, but I think we were maybe behind deadline and there were still piles of sports results to get out, or something.

'Anyway, Boothby was holding court when, suddenly, the pressure got too much for one of our subs, Andrew Ingram. He stood up and blew his stack. "Look," he said. "I don't know who the bloody hell you think you are, but if you don't get the bloody hell out of our sight, there won't be a paper." He sat down again and WV just steered Boothby quickly and quietly from the room. Nothing more was said.'

William Veitch remained on the board after his retirement. When he died in 1975, he had served 65 years with the Aberdeen papers.

MONEY grew tighter at

LEFT
The Coronation of 1953 gave almost every city, town and village in Scotland an excuse for celebration. This was the contribution in Inverness.

RIGHT
The burgh works department at Huntly assembled an award-winning Coronation display.

Aberdeen Journals from the mid-1950s. Press and Journal circulation had been drifting downwards gently since the end of World War II. It had not been an alarming decline — from 99,000 to 89,000 — but it had persisted unchecked for so long that by the last years of the Fifties, the Aberdeen papers were underperforming badly. Although newsprint was no longer restricted and Lord Kemsley supported all his papers as stoutly as ever, concern about Aberdeen became crisis.

'To be perfectly blunt, we were spending money we weren't making,' said Ken Peters, then Press and Journal Editor. 'I don't believe the staff got wind of the crisis, for I don't remember them being anything other than as cheery and professional as usual, but the board knew that we were in a very serious situation, indeed.

'The papers were as good as ever they had been, and our circulation figures on the Press and Journal were still relatively good for the time, although not as good as they had been during the war. But costs are always the difficulty in newspapers; it's a high-cost industry, and our costs had been rising and revenue not keeping pace until all of us in senior management could see the buffers coming. It wasn't a question *if.* It was a matter *when.'*

The solution lay not in Aberdeen. It did not lie in Scotland. It was not even to be found in Britain. The answer to the latest of many Press and Journal financial crises came from across the Atlantic.

Roy Thomson was a Canadian-Scot with a deep love for the old country. His family was of poor farming stock, and he had failed as a farmer in Saskatchewan, then had gone bankrupt in business. Almost penniless, he had bought into a ramshackle Canadian radio station in the middle of the Depression, despite the fact that he knew nothing about broadcasting.

His nickel-and-dime station survived on loans, overdrafts and postponed salary cheques for long enough until the industry and the Canadian economy stabilised. Gradually, he added other stations to his operation. Then he expanded into weekly newspapers. He bought his first in Timmins, Ontario, for $200 in 1934. So quickly did he turn round this loss-maker that he was encouraged to try again.

He went to the bank in Timmins and drew 100 dimes from his personal account. He went home and pulled out a map of North America, looking for 100 towns the size of Timmins (population then about 15,000). He found out the name and address of each town's newspaper, then sent each editor a dime, asking for a copy of the paper by return mail.

When the papers began arriving, he spread out each side by side and began a personal project to analyse the strengths and weaknesses of small-town weeklies. Effectively, he was teaching himself newspapers.

He came to exactly the same conclusions as the management of the Free Press had done in Aberdeen almost a century earlier: to beat the competition, you publish more often. Roy Thomson acquired several more weeklies and began converting them into bi-weeklies or dailies. When he had bought every

BELOW
The Queen inspects her first Ballater guard.

RIGHT
Neither Dyce nor Dalcross. The Press and Journal's first papers by air flew from Kintore.

A9
KINGUSSIE
(A 96)
RESTAURANT
CAPSTAN
RESTAURANT
A. GRANT
FRASER & McCOLL
FRASER McCOLL
GORDONS FOR SWEETS FLOWERS
SANDEMAN
FRUITS
THE CENTRAL FRUIT STORE
CENTRAL
CHEMIST
SCOTLAND ENGLAND
ERF
SHELL
BP
Leyland
KST 648
GST 625
DUS 803
JST 353
TLD 956
JST 693

LEFT
Busy Inverness on September 7, 1957.

RIGHT
One of the giants of the Press and Journal. William Veitch was an Edinburgh man who worked for the Broad Street papers for 65 years, as London bureau chief, Editor and Editor-in-chief.

weekly that was ripe for sale, he moved into established dailies.

By the late 1940s, Roy Thomson was Canada's biggest media magnate, and his ambitions had outgrown the vastness of his country. Every North American newspaper-owner who wanted to sell thought first of Thomson, but these approaches were not coming quickly enough or often enough for Thomson's liking.

On a visit to Britain in 1952, he declared to a group of journalists at a press conference at Claridges Hotel that he dreamed of owning a newspaper or two in Britain. In a subsequent private conversation with fellow-Canadian press baron Lord Beaverbrook, he was pressed to say which British newspapers he would particularly like to own.

'The Aberdeen ones,' he said. 'I like the look of 'em.'

Later, in the Bahamas, Beaverbrook questioned Thomson incessantly about the state of the North American newspaper market, and Thomson questioned Beaverbrook about likely openings in Britain. Beaverbrook did not urge Thomson to invest in British newspapers but, more important for Roy Thomson, he had specifically not discouraged it, which Thomson, being Thomson, took as encouragement.

In early 1952, he arranged to have himself invited to Lord Kemsley's home at Dropmore, Buckinghamshire.

The welcome was not as warm as it might have been. Apart from a handshake on arrival and conversation at mealtimes, Thomson recalled later, he spent hardly any time in Lord Kemsley's company. Instead, Lord Kemsley had asked his young assistant, Denis Hamilton, to look after 'this Canadian hillbilly'.

After lunch, Denis Hamilton was assigned to escort Thomson round the mansion's magnificent grounds and Hamilton was intrigued to find that the Canadian could not have cared less about the shrubbery and lawns. Instead, Thomson was probing gently to see if the Aberdeen papers might be for sale.

Hamilton met Lord Kemsley shortly before dinner and explained the set of Thomson's mind. Kemsley discussed the matter with Thomson briefly over pre-dinner drinks 'with no warmth at all', Denis Hamilton recalled later. 'All Lord Kemsley told him was that any Kemsley paper could be bought at the right price, and that if Roy was serious, I, as Lord Kemsley's assistant would pass him Lord Kemsley's decision later.'

Several days later, Thomson received a summons to meet Hamilton. It made quite a meeting. Here was an informal, bluff Canadian business magnate called to meet a formal, reserved Englishman 25 years his junior.

'So, did he fix a price?' asked Thomson excitedly.

'Yes.'

'How much?'

'Two million pounds.'

There was silence for half a minute while Thomson realised that he was being delivered a calculated snub by Lord Kemsley, through an emissary.

The Aberdeen papers' financial performance was unknown to Thomson, but he knew enough about newspapers to know that even the best-performing regional dailies were not worth £2million. He had not expected the price to break £500,000.

'What you're saying, Denis,' said Thomson slowly, 'is that they're not for sale.'

'A fair inference.'

'But, if I recall, Kemsley said that any of his papers was for sale.'

'At a price,' said Hamilton with a faint hint of a smile.

Thomson returned to Toronto.

LEFT
Ballater, 1959. The Queen Mother, Prince Charles and Princess Anne chat with locals.

BELOW
1961. The proof-readers: last defence against errors.

THE following year, Thomson bought the Scotsman, knowing that the owners, the Findlay family, would shortly be crippled by death duties and that the Scotsman as a newspaper would suffer as the family struggled to pay the debt. The knowledge strengthened his negotiating hand and, subject to a clause that Thomson would never sell the paper to an Englishman or English company, the Findlays sold their company.

'He's flipped his lid,' his daughter Irma said. 'He is the biggest thing in Canadian newspapers and he's taken on a dead dog in Scotland.'

Thomson did not appear to be worried that the Scotsman was a dead dog. He admitted to liking what he saw as prestige and hoped that it would earn him a knighthood within a couple of years. Besides, he knew how to turn round a loss-maker.

He settled in well to Edinburgh society. Once, when he was presented to the Queen Mother at Holyroodhouse, she remarked that she had heard that the new owner of the Scotsman was Canadian. 'By birth, ma'am,' he said, 'but don't let the accent fool you. I'm a Scot now.'

'How splendid for you,' said Her Majesty.

Next, Thomson turned his attentions to another medium. ITV had been born in the English Home Counties in 1955 and had been struggling to cover its start-up costs. When the Independent Television Authority announced competitive tendering for a station for Central Scotland, Thomson became interested.

Knowing that he needed as much Scottish backing as possible, he tugged the elbows of as many of his new contacts in Scottish society as possible, encouraging them to invest with him in the licence bid. Virtually all turned him down. He was rejected by, among hundreds of others, the Scottish Labour Party, Sir Hugh Fraser, several lords, half a dozen minor aristocrats, Sir

Harold Yarrow, the Lord Provost of Aberdeen, Outrams, a dozen MPs, the Scottish Co-operative movement and Lord Beaverbrook.

Of the few who did back him, one was Jimmy Logan, the entertainer, who put up £1,000. Another was John Profumo, still untainted by the scandal which would descend about him seven years later. Roy Thomson was highly impressed for years later that Jimmy Logan had had the business acumen to see the opportunities in television, while so many established magnates had cried off.

He won the licence, and was on hand when STV opened on August 31, 1957, with the words: 'This is Scotland.'

Unlike their wary counterparts south of the Border, advertisers in the Central Belt were entranced by the new medium and demand became so great that there was scarcely enough airtime to sell. Within months, revenue was flowing into STV at such a rate that Thomson turned to an associate and uttered the most famous quote in British TV history: 'Owning a TV station is a licence to print money.'

By now a key player in two divisions of Scottish media, Thomson felt sufficiently secure to turn again to his first and dearest ambition, Aberdeen. He arranged a lunch with Lord

Two Canadian press barons together. Lord Thomson (left) and Lord Beaverbrook share a joke at Lord Beaverbrook's 85th birthday party at the Dorchester — arranged and paid for by Lord Thomson.

Kemsley in London in early 1958. Kemsley did not wait for social niceties. His first words to Thomson were: 'I know what you want. You want Aberdeen.'

'Among others,' said Thomson.

'It's yours for two and a half million,' said Kemsley.

By now, the Aberdeen papers' financial position was even worse than it had been six years earlier. The Weekly Journal had been shut in 1957 because the public had felt it was too similar in tone and content to the Press and Journal and Evening Express and had stopped buying. That had ended a 209-year run of weekly-paper production.

So Thomson knew that £2.5million in 1958 was just as much a snub as £2million had been in 1952.

'Aberdeen turns in barely a hundred thousand a year,' Thomson pointed out.

'I know,' said Kemsley.

'And you still want two and a half million?'

'Yes.'

'Then you still don't want to sell, do you?'

Kemsley just smiled.

The seven-year impasse persisted for many months until, in July, 1959, Thomson took a call at his Edinburgh desk. It was Kemsley. 'Roy I want to see you.'

'Fine, I happen to be in London next week.'

'Sooner, if possible.'

'Friday, then.'

'Can't you come down tonight? When I tell you what I want to discuss, you'll consider it serious.'

Thomson caught the sleeper to King's Cross and checked in at the Savoy. He took a taxi to Kemsley House in Gray's Inn Road, where Kemsley welcomed him formally, but wasted no time.

'Roy, I'm going to say to you something I never thought I'd say to anybody. I'm going to offer you the Kemsley papers. I've got 40% of the shares. I want £6 a share for myself and for any minority shareholders who might want to sell.'

Thomson knew that Kemsley shares were valued at £2 2/- on the Stock Exchange. If he bought, he would be paying £15million for a group judged to be worth a little more than £5million. Even allowing for the fact that the Sunday Times would be part of the deal, as well as the coveted Aberdeen operation, the price was too steep.

'Beyond me,' said Thomson bluntly.

Lord Kemsley suggested that Thomson go to see his bankers, while Lord Kemsley saw his. Something could be worked out, Kemsley was sure.

Nine days of discussion followed. During the negotiations, Thomson stayed at the Savoy (£6 15/- a night) but he had breakfast in a lorry drivers' café across the road. As he explained to his right-hand-man, Jim Coltart later: 'I've never seen the point in wasting money.'

Kemsley dropped to £5 a share, which put the company closer to Thomson's grasp, but still not quite close enough.

Then both sides fixed on a deal staggering in its simplicity. It was the first recorded example of what the City has come to know as a reverse bid. Instead of Thomson buying Kemsley, Kemsley would buy STV, paying Thomson with Kemsley shares of such voting power that Thomson would then control the combined Kemsley/STV.

That way, Thomson would spend only £5million for Kemsley's 40%. There was a risk if the minority shareholders wanted out, for Thomson could not afford to buy their shares, but he was enough of a gambler to know that the risk was small, and that, once they realised who was the new man in charge, most would want to ride along.

The deal was cleared by the bankers and by the ITA and so, seven years after failing to buy Aberdeen at the first attempt, and failing at the second in January, 1958, Thomson found that he owned one of the biggest newspaper groups in the United Kingdom; had become one of his adopted country's Big Four newspaper barons overnight and, best of all, at last owned Aberdeen.

He put out a statement to the media almost at once: 'The newspapers of this group published outside London serve some of the most important and flourishing regions in Britain. Each of these papers — including the Press and Journal — has, for many years, played an important role in the communal life of its area, recording, interpreting and influencing, nowhere more so than in the northern half of Scotland.

'I intend to ensure, so far as I can, that these papers will not only continue to play that role, but will be encouraged and supported in expanding and developing it so that they might keep pace with — indeed, lead — the expansion and development of their communities.

'The primary responsibility rests with the editors, and it has always been my policy with my editors to give them the greatest possible freedom of action to further the interests of their communities and their papers.'

He was as good as his word. From 1959 until 1995, it always

LIBBY'S ARCADE OF VALUES
SPECIAL "DIVI" BAG
1lb. Corned Beef
1 Pineapple Grapefruit Drink
1 Large Milk
1 Large Tin Pine Tidbits
1 Box Cheemello Cheese
6/8 VALUE
FOR 6/-
FULL DIVIDEND WITH EVERY OFFER!
FOR 3/4
FREE COMPETITION WITH EVERY PURCHASE
Milk

LEFT
A busy Saturday morning at the old Loch Street Co-opie Arcade in Aberdeen.

RIGHT
Said to be Lord Thomson's favourite photograph of himself as a press baron — a publicity still from an hour-long profile made by the National Film Board of Canada.

amused journalists at Broad Street when rivals tried to make capital of the supposed Canadian ownership of the Press and Journal and Evening Express. During Roy Thomson's ownership, there was less proprietorial interference in the running of Broad Street than there was in many Scottish-owned papers, particularly the Glasgow Herald.

Roy Thomson encouraged freedom of thought and action and, on several occasions, was delighted when several of his papers took an editorial line against multi-media ownership, for it showed independence of spirit, and he liked that.

In 1965, shortly after he was made Baron Thomson of Fleet, he declared: 'A newspaper proprietor has one supreme responsibility. He must ensure that his newspapers follow two basic principles. The first is that they should be operated in the best interests of the communities they serve. The second is that they should tell the truth and report all happenings accurately and without bias.

'A newspaper cannot be free unless it is viable. When I insist that newspapers should be profitable, this is no more than saying that an editor cannot do his job with the fearless integrity which is his duty if he is forever glancing over his shoulder to

wonder whether or not the newspaper will come out the next week.'

ROY THOMSON had bought Aberdeen, but he had little idea of the state of the company, the standard of the premises or the morale of the staff. He called for a full report in December, 1959. This became known as The Pratt Report and one yellowing copy still exists in Press and Journal company archives. It paints a fascinating picture of Aberdeen Journals' health at the time.

Profits of £160,000 in 1956 had halved to £80,000 in 1957, and then had collapsed to £28,000 in 1958. For the turnover and effort involved, these profits were abysmal.

The Press and Journal cost $2\frac{1}{2}$d and was selling 89,000 a day. The Evening Express was 3d and was selling 85,000.

The company had laid down a complicated distribution network during the 1950s, buying a fleet of vans to strike into all points of northern Scotland. It was also among the first British newspaper companies to use scheduled air services for paper deliveries.

'But,' said the Pratt Report, 'there does not appear to be any prospect of a vast increase in revenue, so it is necessary to examine every item of expenditure carefully. Among its many observations and recommendations, some scathing and damning, were:

'The office consists of three old buildings on different levels, which doesn't make for maximum efficiency. Generally speaking, however, the flow of copy has been well thought-out and is streamlined.

'The public portion of the office is deplorable. It is dingy and dismal and certainly does not create a desire in the public to bring in classified advertisements. In addition to this, the publishing department is badly sited. Night and day, four men transport papers from the folding machines to the packing tables. In addition to a tendency to smudge wet ink, there seems to be unnecessary labour employed.

'The two editors are young and keen. They have been told of the need for economies and informed that the Editorial expense account for the first nine months of 1959 had risen by 28% and the telephone bill by 18%. They were somewhat staggered

ABOVE
Keith battens down the hatches for a dreich Christmas in the 1960s

RIGHT
Shopping for drapery in pounds, shillings and pence.

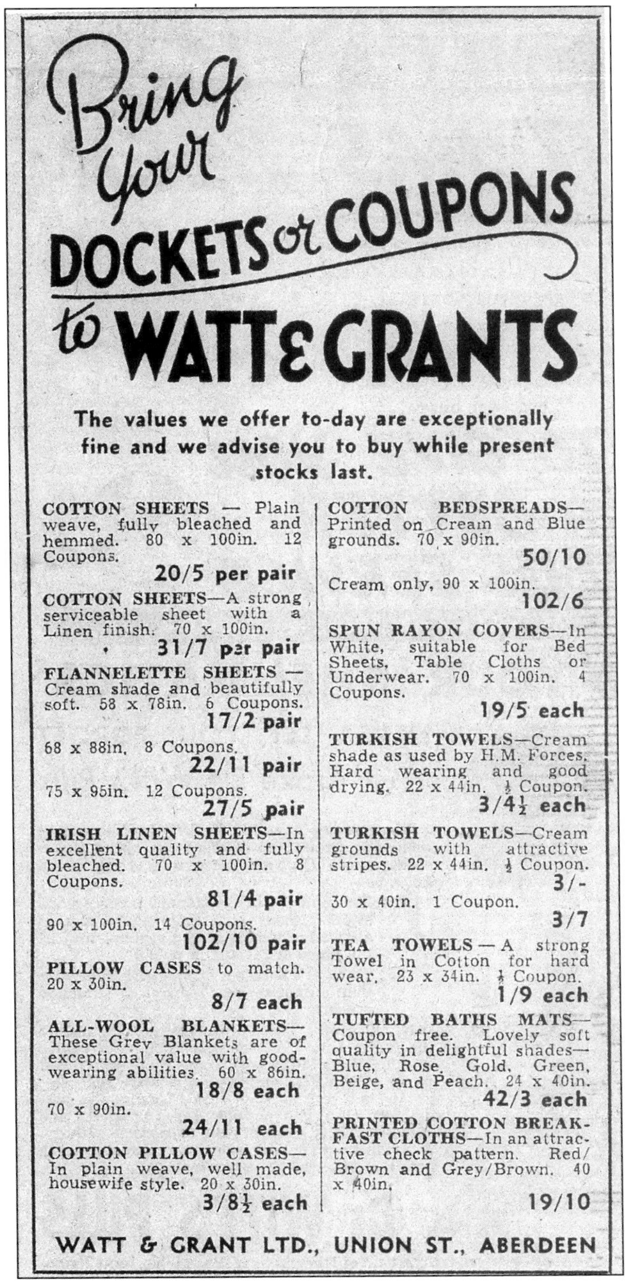

by these figures and there is no doubt they will co-operate to the full. Generally speaking, Editorial is not overstaffed.

Bring Your
DOCKETS or COUPONS
to WATT & GRANTS
The values we offer to-day are exceptionally fine and we advise you to buy while present stocks last.
COTTON SHEETS — Plain weave, fully bleached and hemmed. 80 x 100in. 12 Coupons.
20/5 per pair
COTTON SHEETS—A strong serviceable sheet with a Linen finish. 70 x 100in.
31/7 per pair
FLANNELETTE SHEETS — Cream shade and beautifully soft. 58 x 78in. 6 Coupons.
17/2 pair
68 x 88in. 8 Coupons.
22/11 pair
75 x 95in. 12 Coupons.
27/5 pair
IRISH LINEN SHEETS—In excellent quality and fully bleached. 70 x 100in. 8 Coupons.
81/4 pair
90 x 100in. 14 Coupons.
102/10 pair
PILLOW CASES to match. 20 x 30in.
8/7 each
ALL-WOOL BLANKETS—These Grey Blankets are of exceptional value with good-wearing abilities. 60 x 86in.
18/8 each
70 x 90in.
24/11 each
COTTON PILLOW CASES—In plain weave, well made, housewife style. 20 x 30in.
3/8½ each
COTTON BEDSPREADS—Printed on Cream and Blue grounds. 70 x 90in.
50/10
Cream only, 90 x 100in.
102/6
SPUN RAYON COVERS—In White, suitable for Bed Sheets, Table Cloths or Underwear. 70 x 100in. 4 Coupons.
19/5 each
TURKISH TOWELS—Cream shade as used by H.M. Forces. Hard wearing and good drying. 22 x 44in. ½ Coupon.
3/4½ each
TURKISH TOWELS—Cream grounds with attractive stripes. 22 x 44in. ½ Coupon.
3/-
30 x 40in. 1 Coupon.
3/7
TEA TOWELS — A strong Towel in Cotton for hard wear. 23 x 34in. ½ Coupon.
1/9 each
TUFTED BATHS MATS—Coupon free. Lovely soft quality in delightful shades—Blue, Rose, Gold, Green, Beige, and Peach. 24 x 40in.
42/3 each
PRINTED COTTON BREAKFAST CLOTHS—In an attractive check pattern. Red/Brown and Grey/Brown. 40 x 40in.
19/10
WATT & GRANT LTD., UNION ST., ABERDEEN

'There is an extensive library which seems to be out of proportion to the demands of the office.

'Costs in the works department seem to be very high. Maintenance in production departments, which costs £10,171 annually at the Middlesbrough centre, costs £33,831 in Aberdeen.

'As to circulation, this is some of the most difficult territory in the British Isles. Editions are changed four times a night to give local editions. There are 15,000 postal copies every night. There are two branch offices, at Inverness and Elgin.

'There are 31 cars and 18 vans, kept in a garage two miles away from the Broad Street office.

'Staffing in the Works department seems exceptionally heavy. Where Middlesbrough manages with 10, Aberdeen has 30, including a doorman and a fireman.'

When staff got wind of the Pratt Survey and the reason behind it, they became a good deal more agitated than their predecessors had been during the Berry takeover in 1928.

They were not confident that Aberdeen Journals was sufficiently tightly run for the Canadian magnate who, they knew, ran such a tight ship. Even so, they were not prepared for the gravity of the news when the scale of waste and overmanning became apparent.

The deputy managing director of the Thomson Group drew managers and trade-union representatives into the Broad Street board room and outlined the scale of the problem.

'The Press and Journal might look healthy in circulation terms,' he said, 'but it has been losing money for years, and I think we're now at the point when the Evening Express cannot carry its elder brother any longer.'

For the second time in 80 years, Aberdeen's morning paper was perilously close to being closed. When Roy Thomson read the recommendations, he sent word north that he would have to see one or two of Aberdeen's senior people as soon as possible. He disliked shutting newspapers, especially ones, such as the Press and Journal, which were performing so well editorially, but so badly financially.

When Press and Journal Editor Ken Peters arrived on the executive floor at Thomson's HQ in Gray's Inn Road, London, the Canadian fixed him with a stare. Thomson's opening line was: 'Don't you guys know how to live like Aberdonians?'

CHAPTER VI

Jimmy Grant's Plan

IF JAMES CHALMERS conceived the idea of a newspaper for the North of Scotland, it was Jimmy Grant, two centuries later, who saved it from collapse and extinction. Without question, these two Moravians are key figures in 250 years of the paper's history.

Had there been no Jimmy Grant in the 1960s, the Press and Journal would not have survived.

Its new owner, Roy Thomson, had been horrified by his first trawl through the Aberdeen Journals balance sheet. The Press and Journal's circulation was low for a daily paper at the time, and unchecked spending and overmanning in every department except Accounts and Editorial was sapping what little strength the company had.

Thomson told two of his board at an angry private meeting late in 1959 that he did not understand how any manager could allow a company with such potential to drift towards the rocks and do nothing at the rudder.

If Roy Thomson was moved to anger when he discovered what problems he had bought, he was typically calm by the time he summoned Press and Journal Editor Ken Peters to London for discussions. Those discussions amounted to offering Ken the critical position of General Manager. But with promotion came grave responsibility, and Ken Peters knew it even before Thomson had finished delivering his formal offer. Then came the punch.

'Ya got two years,' said Thomson, face without expression.

Ken Peters took the night sleeper back to Aberdeen, but he had very little sleep. In ordinary circumstances, General Manager was an important promotion, but this one had the faint whiff of poisoned chalice.

Ken's euphoria mingled with foreboding. He was a journalist. His business experience was limited to what he had picked up in dealings with his commercial colleagues at the paper. As editor of first the Evening Express and then the Press and Journal

James Currie Grant, Editor of the Press and Journal from 1960 to 1975, dressed in typically dapper style and in the hot seat he loved so much.

The staff of the Press and Journal in the 1960s and 1970s were some of the finest journalists the northern half of Scotland has produced. Now retired, former chief reporter Ethel Simpson describes these decades as the heyday of the paper. Here, staff are assembled to say farewell to editorial driver Willie Macdonald (front row third left). Jimmy Grant is seated fifth left.

during the 1950s, he had certainly developed good and trusted contacts throughout the North of Scotland, but good business contacts alone don't rescue a company.

On the day he returned, he set about a series of meetings with the company's senior managers to assess the task ahead and explain Roy Thomson's ultimatum. They were as alarmed — almost resigned — as he, and knew the ultimatum was not negotiable.

Not one of them doubted that the threat of closure was sincere and real. Fond though Thomson had declared he was of owning Scottish papers, he was no sentimentalist when it came to business, and the prospect of the North of Scotland without its own daily paper was suddenly crystallised.

The loneliness of command had never been more apparent at Aberdeen Journals as Ken Peters surveyed the boardroom that afternoon, but his first move was obvious. While he set about staunching the commercial losses, he needed a strong editor to pilot the company albatross, the Press and Journal.

JIMMY GRANT might never have been a journalist. There was no journalism in his family. He had no great notions of journalism as a career. He was a good scholar at a time when Elgin Academy had many good scholars.

The pivot of Jimmy's life came when the editor of the Moray and Nairn Gazette arrived at the academy one afternoon in 1930 to speak to senior pupils. He described his job and the responsibilities which went with it. Then, after answering questions, began asking a few of his own.

Which of them were good at writing? Who had the best marks in grammar, spelling and punctuation? And which, if any, would like a job as a journalist?

The successful candidate was Jimmy Grant.

It was a baptism of fire. Within months of Jimmy's arrival in journalism, his editor became gravely ill and was hospitalised for long periods. Still a teenager, Jimmy had to assume more and more of the editorial burden until, within a year, he was virtually editing a weekly newspaper single-handedly at a time when many of his school contemporaries were still finding their feet at university.

Instead of resenting the imposition or fearing the responsibility, he relished the challenge. More than 40 years later, he would tell a businessmen's dinner in Aberdeen Town House that there was no such thing as a problem, only an opportunity and a solution. His spell in the hot seat as Elgin's teenage editor was the

LEFT
Press and Journal vans became an increasingly familiar sight around the North and North-east as the paper's circulation climbed from the doldrums.

RIGHT
The wire room, on the Broad Street top floor, was one of the few workplaces in the building with natural light. Today's equipment occupies a space less than one-sixth of this.

ANS SIT-DOWN
TO FIRING BY
ICE
MR

first example of the Grant philosophy in action.

Having been inspired by the excitement of editorship, Jimmy now sought broader horizons. In 1936, he moved to the Press and Journal to work for the paper in the Central Belt as a reporter. A good reporter, too, by accounts; hungering for action.

He was just getting into his stride and making a name for himself with his superiors when war broke out.

He enlisted in the Royal Artillery, spending most of his six years in India and returning to find that the only job open to him at the Journals was on the Press and Journal sub-editors desk. He accepted, and the second pivot of his career was fixed.

Over five post-war years, he made steady progress through the sub-editors' ranks until, in 1953, he was made deputy editor to George Ley Smith. Given Mr Smith's long and protracted illnesses, Jimmy was *de facto* Editor more often than not until his boss stepped down finally in 1956, for health reasons. Ken Peters, then Evening Express editor, transferred to the morning paper to become Jimmy's boss.

But the paper was already showing signs of decline and stagnation. Circulation was fading steadily. By 1959, no matter which of many ploys management and senior editorial staff tried, they were crewing a newspaper lumbering from crisis to catastrophe, seemingly irrecoverable and, unknown to the rank-and-file staff, losing around £60,000 a year, a colossal sum for a regional newspaper company.

Jimmy's big chance came at the end of 1959, when Roy Thomson saw business skills in Ken Peters and removed him from Editorial to give him overall commercial responsibility for the whole of Aberdeen Journals. At once, the Editor's seat at the Press and Journal was temptingly empty.

'I proposed that Jimmy Grant was the obvious candidate to take over from me as Editor,' Ken Peters said later, 'there was no dissent at London HQ, but I recall being taken to one side and asked if I thought someone might ask Jimmy to smarten up a bit if he was to be Editor.

'Subs have never been known for their fashion statements, of course. I can't remember how I broached the subject with him, but I must have done, because the transformation was remarkable. That was the start of thirty years of loud suits, fancy waistcoats and bow ties. You've never seen such a change in a man's wardrobe.'

Hilda Grant, Jimmy's wife, has different memories. 'He was always a smart dresser,' she said. 'He liked to take a pride in his

As the need grew for intensely local news, news telephonists, or copy-takers, became increasingly important. Stories were phoned in by amateur correspondents and reporters on assignment. Here, Elma Glennie takes a story from reporter Ted Strachan in 1961.

ABOVE RIGHT
A 1962 publicity shot involving the transport department.

BELOW
As circulation grew, ever more copies of the Press and Journal came hot from the Broad Street presses.

appearance, but he certainly became snappier as the years wore on.

'He would buy a bolt of cloth that he liked the look of and he'd have suits made up in town. He wanted special care with the way the trousers fell. He liked them tapered to different lengths front and back so that the creases were just so. That's the kind of man he was.'

Hilda recalls the day Jimmy was offered the editorship. 'He wasn't an ambitious man in the sense that he would have trampled on other people for promotion, but he wanted to do what he could for his paper, and he was sure that he could help to turn the Press and Journal round, given the chance. He didn't need long to think about it, put it that way. He jumped at the offer, even although he knew he was taking on the job at probably the deepest crisis in the paper's history.'

Jimmy's solution to that crisis was simple.

Local news.

The Press and Journal had spent years giving the same diet of news to every reader throughout half of Scotland, whether in Inverness, Inverurie or Inverbervie.

Editionising for region was unheard of until Jimmy reasoned that readers would be more inclined to buy the paper if they were assured of a regular diet of news from their own areas.

As a journalist by training, the new general manager, Ken Peters, could see the sense and agreed that it was a radical plan, but worth a shot.

To have the man in charge of the company on your side was to have the wind at your back, Jimmy Grant said later. 'We both understood the strategy — and we both had the two-year ultimatum hanging over us.'

But there were doubts among some commercial colleagues. 'Why would anyone in a small village want to buy a paper to read about something they know, anyway?' one manager is said to have asked.

'Aye,' agreed Jimmy, 'they probably do know, but they'll read the paper to see fa's been caught at it.'

He was right.

In a frenzy of editionising in 1960 and 1961, he split the North of Scotland eventually into seven distinct geographical areas, insisting that his staff do their utmost to focus down on those areas and give each what amounted to its own daily paper.

Reporters were to look for distinctly local stories. A network of amateur correspondents would be built and asked to keep alert for newsy snippets in towns and villages, hamlets and parishes across the North and North-east. Sub-editors were to present stories in a way which emphasised their local importance. Thus grew the Press and Journal's popular image as an obsessively parish-pump daily paper; Jimmy Grant could not have cared less.

'If, by parish-pump news, you mean that it was news that people in the smallest places wanted to read,' he told a retirement-dinner assembly in 1979, 'then I plead guilty. There is no shame in giving people what they want, and what they wanted was news about themselves. Still do. And the paper that fancies it is above that

The Press and Journal

is a paper which is being written for itself, not for its readers. Give me parish pump every time. The Press and Journal knows better than any other regional paper that that is what works.'

Conveying this belief to his staff in 1960 was not at all difficult.

'I want local news, treated locally,' he once told his sub-editors. 'I want placenames. I want the names of even the smallest villages and hamlets as high up a story as possible. I want placenames in headings. I want people to know that this is their paper. I want them to know it's a paper with news for *them*.'

The dividends were not long in coming.

Well within Roy Thomson's two-year deadline, Aberdeen Journals was turning in a handsome profit. While the healthy circulation of the Evening Express remained steady, the once-floundering Press and Journal increased by an average 4,000 a year — an increase inconceivable nowadays.

Within three years, Jimmy Grant's recipe saw the Press and Journal break the sustained 100,000 mark for the first time, and the climb continued until the mid-1970s, when the paper topped out at a regular 117,450. By the time Jimmy retired, after 15 years in the hot seat, he was leaving a paper selling 20,000 more daily copies as on the day he had taken over; a company making substantial money on the back of the highest sales in more than 200 years, and a staff of journalists so devoted and loyal to him that some were in tears at his retirement dinner.

HILDA GRANT smiled, then laughed. 'Oh, he could be an irritable bugger at times. I don't want to give the impression he was a complete saint. But I don't think he ever really brought his problems home with him, even although he must have been under tremendous pressure, especially in the first year or two.

'He used to walk home from Broad Street to Ferryhill for lunchtimes and his few hours at home in the afternoon before his night work. I suppose he would have been churning office problems in his mind during the walk. But by the time he came through the front door, he must have had them sorted out. He was perfectly calm. We never suffered for the difficulties at work.'

Duncan MacRae, who retired as Highland Editor in 1996, has vivid memories of his first Jimmy Grant encounter.

'I had moved from the North Star, Dingwall, to go to college in Aberdeen to improve my shorthand and typing. I'd gone into Broad Street on the offchance that there might be an opening and they took my name. I had digs in King Street and a job as an usher at the Playhouse Cinema near Holburn Junction. You become well-versed in films when you're an usher.

'Anyway, one day in 1955 a messenger arrived and asked me to go and see Jimmy Grant about a job. Jimmy was running the paper because the editor, George Ley Smith, was off ill.

' "We'll put you in subs for a trial week," said Jimmy.

'I was a reporter. I had never sub-edited other writers' copy before. But I wasn't going to pass up a chance to get a foot in the door, so I just asked Jimmy: "But what do I do?"

' "Subbing?" he said. "What do you do? Nothing to it. Anybody could manage. You can work in my office for the week and we'll see if you shape up. If you're any good, we'll put you through with the rest of them."

'By the end of the first week I had no real idea of what I'd been doing or how well I'd been doing it, so I went to him at the end of my last shift and asked what would be happening now.

' "Ach," he said, "just go through next week."

'So that was that. Occasionally, I'd ask him about a reporter's job, which was what I really wanted, but he would always

LEFT
As circulation rose, demand for delivery boys and girls grew. Here Inverness teenagers in 1962 take over in the last stage of the journey from newsroom to living-room.

Magic Secret

The Press and Journal

VENETIAN BLINDS

Archibalds

Aberdeen's tourist trade could be hit as...

TYPHOID TOTAL RISES TO 75

Latest typhoid cases named

City hotels are losing bookings

THE SOURCE: MOH ANSWERS CRITICS

3 Fs OF SCOTS SCHOOLING—BY A MINISTER

MOUNTAIN DEATHS INQUIRY

Highland trench tragedy

Tons of rubble cave in on Dalcross man

CANCELLED

UNHAPPY

QUIET

Teacher ill on the Cairngorms

Millie in hospital

Cordiners

150 FINE USED CARS

ALL THE NEW FORDS

BRI NYLON

ESSLEMONT & MACINTOSH

DOCTOR HURT IN CRASH

MIDNIGHT WEATHER

Sunny

NORTH KEEPS COOL, BUT N.E. BASKS IN SUN

say: "When one comes up, we'll let you know."

'I never did get it.'

Duncan moved in February, 1960, to the Scottish Daily Express in Glasgow. 'I wanted a change and the Express was looking for people. I quite enjoyed my time down there, but nobody was really expected to stay long. Then I decided to get married and I didn't really want to settle in Glasgow, so I called Jimmy less than a year later and said I was thinking of coming back.

' "Will you have me?"

' "We'll think about it," was all he said.

' "I couldn't come back on my old salary, of course," I said.

' "Is that so?"

'Anyway, I moved back to the Press and Journal in April, 1960, at £18 a week, with a letter from Jimmy saying he was sure I would find conditions 'as happy as before. We have a very fine team and hope to notch our century of sales (100,000) very soon.'

'The changes Jimmy had made in my time away hit me at once. From doing half a dozen pages a night in the Fifties, suddenly we were doing 12 or 16. Some of the old faces had retired and new people were in the top jobs. I remember noticing that the top three men, Jimmy Grant, Sandy Meston and George Inglis, used to read all the page proofs and do all their own lawyering; no lifting the phone to have a story legalled. To the best of my memory, they didn't put a foot wrong.

'There was more editionising. Jimmy had started editionising like mad. There was a P and J for Caithness and Sutherland. There was one for Ross-shire. Every county seemed to have its own paper, and to feed all of that we'd had to develop an active network of freelances. It was a demanding regime and hard work, but there's no question that the recipe worked. There's no doubt in my mind that that's what rescued the Press and Journal. That and sheer hard work with Jimmy at the head of the team.'

Ethel Simpson, former Press and Journal chief reporter and one of Scotland's first women journalists, agrees: 'Editors had to do more and more reports for the commercial side as the Fifties wore into the Sixties, and they got less and less involved with the paper, but not Jimmy Grant. Jimmy would dash off his commercial reports, then we'd see the jacket come off. He liked to work.

'He was in his element with a big-breaking story. On a night with one of those happening, he would just sit down and take

Aberdeen Medical Officer of Health Dr Ian MacQueen (right) held frequent media briefings to help pilot the city through its worst health crisis.

charge and the whole thing would just gel. You could actually see it happening.'

Jimmy Grant's tenure coincided with two of the biggest-breaking stories, drawing international attention. The first came at 4.45pm on Thursday, May 21, 1964. George Ness answered the phone to hear a tipoff that typhoid had broken out in Aberdeen.

Unusually, the call came not from a contact. It came from the man at the top, the city's Medical Officer of Health (MOH), Dr Ian MacQueen.

A shrewd and hugely likeable man, Dr MacQueen knew that publicity and media co-operation would be vital to defeat what he knew was about to become an epidemic. By making the approach, he built a bond of trust between medicine and media that has not been known since.

'Ian MacQueen and his wife were two of my best contacts,' recalled Pearl Murray, then women's editor. 'He had a wonderful gift for colourful quotes, long before the age of the soundbite. He was eminently approachable and, from a writer's point of view, nothing was too much trouble for him. Considering the stress he must have been under at the time, he was amazing.

'We were definitely a beleaguered city, and, yes, it was scary, but he was wonderfully reassuring. It's thanks to him that there was no mass panic, I'm convinced.'

If there was panic, it came in the foreign media. Several American broadsheets printed an agency report trumpeting that 'Scottish people are dying in the streets!' Almost every major world

Jimmy Grant made five retirement speeches in 1975 and 1976. They give a fascinating insight into his attitudes to his paper, his staff and his profession. Here are highlights from the first and the last — to his Scottish editor peers and to his staff

IT HAS been a hard slog for me. I wouldn't like anyone to think otherwise. Today, the Press and Journal has a good sale and makes money. It seems to me that some papers are luxuries, but the Press and Journal is a necessity to its readers.

As Sir Denis Hamilton has been good enough to tell me on several occasions, if a person comes from Elgin, or Inverness, or John O' Groats or Aberdeen, or anywhere in the northern half of Scotland, he or she should buy the Press and Journal every day and the Sunday Times on Sunday, and be among the best-informed people in the world.

My favourite story about the P and J? Difficult, but I've always liked this one. A helluva blizzard had been blowing in the Highlands and the police were stopping all traffic at Helmsdale. Suddenly, a familiar red van appeared from the Inverness direction, tore through Helmsdale and roared away on the road to the North.

Angry motorists who had been stopped protested to the police. 'Aye,' said a bobby. 'Even the Lord canna stop the P and J goin through.'

The 1950s and 1960s were the great days on the Press and Journal. We were so busy getting out a paper that we hadn't time for union disputes of any kind. Peter Watson will remember particularly the Fridays when we used to give the picture sub his night off. So in addition to planning and laying out the paper and subbing half a dozen stores, I handled all the pix and captions. I had to keep going on a pie and a pint. I don't suppose it did me any harm, either.

But I would like to say this: the Managing-Editorial partnership of Ken Peters and myself — KJP and JCG — is one of the great success stories in the modern history of regional or local newspapers.

There have been tough times, but I remember only the warmth and the happiness; the team spirit that produced the Press and Journal.

And I would gladly have foregone this gold watch had I known that the Press and Journal would have to go up in price to pay for it.

I CAN hardly believe it is all over, or that the strains, worries and responsibilities of editing the Press and Journal for 16 years should have left so little mark on me.

I feel sometimes that we are too modest in our achievements in Aberdeen. The performance of the Press and Journal is one of the great success stories in the modern history of regional or local newspapers.

In 1959, the Press and Journal had lost £60,000. We were given two years to stop the rot. In 1960, when I took over as Editor, we were still struggling to make a go of it. These were rough nights but, looking back, I remember only the good times, the sense of achievement and our ability to laugh at ourselves.

I must be the luckiest editor in the world; all my career, surrounded by a loyal, dedicated team of journalists who could have held their own anywhere. We were honest; we were fair to all sides, and we were always ready to admit when we made mistakes. That's my kind of paper.

We were going places. Proof of this could be seen when Duncan MacRae came back to us from the Daily Express; Jimmy Menzies from the Daily Record, and Bob Gibb from Grampian TV and the Mearns, via the breath test. I used to think that the Editor of the Press and Journal existed for only one purpose — to make farewell presentations to Bob Gibb.

Now just a tattered ragbag of names and events come to memory. I can't mention everyone. It will tend to be those who were warm friends, as well as colleagues. If I miss anyone out, you can always give me another dinner when I will try to make honourable amends.

Ethel Simpson and Pearl Murray: two first-class journalists who were a damn sight better than most men. John Dunbar, sadly under-rated in my view until he was made municipal correspondent of the Press and Journal. Steadfast Jim Kinnaird, who brought the tang of the sea (or was it the fish market?) into the editorial hall. Cuthbert Graham: who will be the four men to replace him when he sheathes his sword and retires to his castle?

There was the great loss of

George Inglis. I had known and admired him as a journalist for nearly 40 years. Then Eric Donald died after such a gallant fight and surviving several serious operations. recently, it was Peter Brown, just a day or two before Christmas.

But after George Inglis, others stepped in to carry the burden of the Press and Journal — Peter Watson, Cameron Bain and Duncan MacRae. Bill Macdonald and Bob Johnston, possibly the slickest team I ever saw operate on the front page. And Bob, all the time dreaming up these wonderful characters from town, farm and fisher port who have become so real to hundreds of thousands of readers of his Donovan Smith column.

I must tell you a story about Bob. A doctor from Aberlour, a Sassenach, wrote to me that he didn't think Donovan Smith very funny. He could write more humorous stuff himself.

At the time, I had an old uncle in hospital in Aberdeen — about 84, I think.

He hailed from Mulben and was Donovan's No.1 fan. So Bob kindly agreed to accompany me to hospital on his next night off.

I told Uncle John and he was in transports. He had the whole ward buzzing with the news. It did him so much good that he was discharged from hospital next day, before he'd ever seen his idol.

I sat down to write to Aberlour and I told the whole story. 'Next time you've somebody really ill, doctor, give him a dose of Donovan Smith. I guarantee that he'll recover within 24 hours.'

I think of Ian Hardie and all those wonderful pictures which photographers of Aberdeen Journals have produced in the 40 years since I first climbed the narrow stairs of Broad Street. I would hate to be asked who had made the greatest contribution to the rise of the Press and Journal — writers and subs or photographers.

Certainly the dedication of one department was matched by the other.

There were those unforgettable sea pictures; the wrecks off our coast. We had three lifeboat disasters — Arbroath, Longhope and Fraserburgh. If you look back the P and J files of 1970, you will see under the heading 'A vast tidal wave of mourners' possibly the most moving collection of pix I have ever seen in a newspaper.

It was a disaster for Fraserburgh, but the Press and Journal reflected on that cold January day our pride in the lifeboat volunteers — in all men who go down to the sea in ships — in a way that I have never seen equalled.

And I remember a terrific shot by David Sutherland, taken as he lay on his belly in mud high above those cliffs at Gardenstown.

There might never be a better picture of a ship in distress, and it sticks in my memory because of the personal risk involved in getting it.

In Sport, we had Alistair Macdonald, doomed with Colin Farquharson to follow the Dons.

Colin might have been a golfer had he not wanted to hit the ball out of sight. He would be far better on a golf course on a Saturday afternoon than finding alibis for the Dons. Gordon Forbes, a powerhouse of work. Bruce McHardy, whose ability to keep sane is the envy of us all. Val Moonie, a very old colleague who has given me the impression that he has not the same high opinion of his abilities as I have.

A special bonus for me tonight is to see so many of my very old friends, headed by the retired list of Sandy Meston, George Fraser, Alex Munro, Jim Gilchrist and Sandy Bisset: all thoroughbreds from the Broad Street stable.

And I must not forget the news telephonists, and take the opportunity to apologise for any past rudeness . . . done under stress, of course.

And through all our price increases, our readers have remained loyal to the Press and Journal. Obviously, they feel they get value for their money.

Finally, we Scots will forgive a man anything, as long as he can do his work. If he's not fit for that, nothing else will win him acclaim.

So that is what gives me most pleasure as I look back: not that I was Editor of the Press and Journal, but that I was thought fit by my colleagues to be the leader of the team.

True to the traditions of journalism, I have already spent this most handsome cheque. It will help to pay for an elegant display and cocktail cabinet, but I will always associate it with the Press and Journal, because pride of place is given to the silver tray, decanter and crystal glasses with which you honoured me when I became a Commander of the British Empire.

All are welcome to come and see it, and to join my wife and me in a drink to the future health and prosperity of my only newspaper love:

The Press and Journal.

The Press and Journal
FOR TOWN AND FARM
THE PRESS AND JOURNAL
THE PRESS AND JOURNAL
HIGHLAND SHOW
Full Reports: Pictures
16,000
of our readers receive a copy by post daily
WHY NOT YOU?
THE PRESS AND JOURNAL
GIVES MOST NEWS ON FARMING

CHAPTER VII

Start Spreading the News

THE medicine Jimmy Grant had prescribed for the near-corpse of the Press and Journal was local news; reporting from village, town and city in its most minute detail. Reflecting the lives of ordinary readers and their communities would take precedence over almost everything else.

Jimmy saw no reason why the activities of WRIs, scout troops and village fundraisers should be subordinate to the pronouncements, business and tastes of politicians, councillors and gentry, as happened in virtually every Scottish daily, post war. The ordinary man, woman and child and their interests would assume the greater importance, for these were the people who were to buy Jimmy's new-look paper.

The philosophy was simple: reader first.

If the thoughts of politicians were to be given space, they were to be covered only in terms of their likely effects on readers. If council debates were to be reported, they were to be reported not to the last hum, haw and smart aside, but only when decisions and their results impinged on readers.

Most sweeping of all, coverage of the social scene of the elite and the privileged evaporated in a matter of weeks. The new regime at Broad Street saw no reason to devote valuable space to the daily doings of a privileged few. The space would be turned over to the daily doings of ordinary readers.

This wholesale change in emphasis was not achieved cleanly. Old Broad Street hands recall clearly the anguished, sometimes furious phone calls and visits from provosts, MPs and councillors demanding to know why a Press and Journal reporter had not covered a supposedly vital exchange in debate or, worse, why the paper had not sent a reporter at all.

Always, the answer was the same, and always, feathers ruffled, the complainer had little option but to withdraw, muttering usually about

LEFT
The Press and Journal bothy was a fixture at the Royal Highland Show every year during the 1950s, 1960s and 1970s.

RIGHT
Boating down Anderson Drive, Aberdeen, after the flash floods of November, 1951.

LEFT
Bob Carter covered Banff and Banffshire for the Press and Journal for more than 30 years.

RIGHT
Busy morning in Dingwall High Street in 1968.

collapsing standards at Aberdeen Journals.

If this shifting outlook at the Press and Journal was plain to those outside the paper, it called for a sea-change in attitudes within. Reporters were expected to rethink their whole approach; how news was defined and how it was to be written.

News-editing changed as newsdesk personnel had to deploy their Broad Street reporting staff differently; had to develop and encourage a vast new network of amateur correspondents in villages and towns throughout Scotland, and had to judge the worth of copy using entirely new criteria.

The change for sub-editors, caseroom and machine-room men was even more pronounced. Not only did the whole emphasis of news pages change, but multiple editions brought multiple deadlines. Now, evenings and early mornings offered almost continual pressure.

But in the middle of all this swirling change, Jimmy Grant knew that nowhere was the burden greater than in the district offices. If the engine of revival was to be local news, the engine would have to run fastest where the paper met its public.

ABERDEEN JOURNALS had maintained a network of satellite offices in the largest towns of northern Scotland since the inter-war years. Reporting staff were based in Inverness, at Elgin, at Banff and in Buchan. All were charged with reflecting these communities and their hinterlands, via the presses of Broad Street, back to the people among whom they lived.

There was an important extra burden. As with the district offices of every newspaper, not only were these staff their paper's ears, they were also their paper's face. To their communities, district-office reporters, advertising reps and circulation staff *were* the Press and Journal, and that brought unseen difficulties and responsibilities. 'It's not an easy thing, to carry out the full duties of a daily-paper journalist in a small town where everyone knows everyone else,' said Bob Carter, who covered Banffshire from 1957 to 1991.

'Every journalist who has covered court has been approached sooner or later by an accused person or the family and asked to overlook a case. You can't, of course; it would be totally against the ethics of the trade and, anyway, it would be more than your job's worth. But try to explain that when you're a district-office reporter in a small town and the people who are

would amaze you nowadays. I remember in 1960 when the Whitehills lifeboat went out looking for a Belgian trawler and lost contact, and I went up to the fish merchant's door to see if I could gather any details.

'He led me round the town going to all the various doors and saying:

' "This is the lad fae the P and J. He wis winderin if ye could tell him aboot . . ." And they did.

'Nobody knew if the lifeboat was safe and they were worried sick, but they spoke to me.

'The lifeboat *was* safe, in fact. It put in at Cromarty the following morning, but nobody had known it at the time, and I'll always remember that one.'

In the midst of tragedy, there were occasional flashes of black humour, too.

Jim Kinnaird recalls visiting the home of a deceased man and sitting uncomfortably while the widow sorted through a shoebox of photographs, going through the entire collection without finding a picture of her late husband.

'Well,' she said, looking up. 'I aye telt him he should get his photie took. Ye nivver ken fan ye'll need it.'

Jim also recalls visiting the home of a kenspeckle Fraserburgh bachelor who had lived with two sisters and who had just died.

Jim had gone to the door to obtain a picture of the dead man. Coincidentally, he was accompanied by town photographer George Wilson, who had been with him on a previous assignment.

On the doorstep, Jim tried to assure one of the sisters that it was common practice for newspapers to publish a suitable picture along with the obituary of a community notable. Persuaded eventually, she invited them to follow her to the parlour.

Jim followed, expecting to be given the pick of photograph albums. Instead, he and George found themselves in the same room as the coffin and corpse.

'There ye are,' she said. 'Tak yer photie. Isn't he like himsel?'

ABOVE
Buckie Harbour , 1965, shortly before discussions began on extending the fish market.

RIGHT
The perils of the sea have featured regularly in the Press and Journal's coverage.

INS.276

THE heavier burden of responsibility in a district office was reflected always in a higher salary, although history does not record any district man agreeing that the differential reflected the extra work.

To compensate, they could always console themselves with the thought that they had greater freedom than their head-office colleagues and could operate more or less as editors in their own right. Most successful district staff have regarded their bailiwicks in highly personal terms, and most journalists contend that that is essential for good district coverage.

But head office must intrude from time to time and a visit from the Editor is always a time for concern. Twas ever thus.

Alastair Bisset, in charge of Moray coverage since the early 1970s, recalled one such visit by Editor Jimmy Grant, not long after Alastair had settled into the Elgin office.

'I remember he was able to teach you lessons about journalism without your ever realising you'd just been given a lesson,' he said.

'We'd gone out to the Gordon Hotel for a spot of lunch and we'd chatted about the newsiness of Moray and what might be done better; where we were strong and where we were weak, and then the time came for us to get up and go. We were heading for the door when I looked back at where we had been sitting and I saw that Jimmy had left his copy of that day's P and J behind.

' "Jimmy," I said, "you've left your paper."

' "Indeed I have," he said.

' "Whenever you go out and about, always take a few spares with you and leave them lying for other people to find and read. You never know how many new readers you might convert to buying." '

THE backbone of district-office journalism, however, was council, court and community, and Bob Carter enjoyed these particularly. 'There were some rare town councils,' he said. 'Today's toothless community councils are a poor substitute.

'Foggie Town Council was a joy to go to, with Frank Anderson as the town clerk — he once set his trousers on fire. Then there was the town clerk of Portknockie, James D.G. McLeod, who would write the minutes before

LEFT
Alastair Bisset has been in charge of the paper's coverage of Elgin and Moray for 25 years, here in an uncharacteristically restful pose in a distillery, mainstay of the Moray economy.

ABOVE
A shameful episode in Aberdeen history: burning the last of the trams at the beach terminus in 1958.

the meeting, then try to steer the debate and the decision to fit his minutes.

'Yes, there were councillors who'd try and take advantage of you, but you had it out with them and it never happened again.

'I remember a debate at Banff Town Council when, believe it or not, the debate somehow worked round to farting. I thought about the tone of the meeting for a day or two, then I wrote a piece saying that the level of discussion and debate was a disgrace to a royal burgh. So it was, and it was also the duty of any paper to report that to the public. The telling thing was that no one attacked me for it.

'The great thing about the old town councils was that they had councillors who knew the area because they had lived in it all their lives. Maybe they weren't people who could express themselves particularly articulately, because that wasn't the way they had been brought up, but they were perfectly able and intelligent men, and you had to try to let the sense of that shine through in your report.

'You also had to cope with some of the marvels of human nature. I remember the provost of one town, who happened to own a small hotel and bar, appearing in court for selling drink to under-age customers. I wrote the report and it appeared. My brother, who did lemonade deliveries, was told by the provost that the pub's regular order was cancelled forthwith.'

According to Bob, the difficulties of being known in a small town were balanced more than adequately by the benefits. Every district-office journalist who puts effort into developing contacts reaps rewards sooner or later.

'I've had Jimmy Millar the bobby knock on my window as he was passing the house to tell me about some incident or other. And I've been driving towards what the newsdesk had told me was a good-going blaze and been waved down by the police coming the other way to tell me: "Dinna bother, Bob. It's jist a henhoose."

'Mind you, I've also slept

RIGHT
Banchory was pictured in 1966 for a feature which declared it had one of the healthiest economies in Scotland.

BELOW
The last train to Ballater, the 8.35pm, prepares to leave Aberdeen Joint Station on February 27, 1966.

YOUR MURPHY DEALERS
TO CAR PARK
RADIO
E. YOUNG
TELEVISION
Murphy
D'AGOSTINO'S
CONFECTIONERS & TOBACCONISTS
COMPLETE HOUSE FURNISHERS
SENIOR SERVICE
SU 913
NLN 640

through the night when the Crown Hotel at the end of my road went on fire. There was all that activity with the police and the fire brigade and the ambulance and I never heard a thing. Sound asleep.

'On the whole, though, if a district-office man puts himself about and attends all the meetings and takes an interest in people, it makes the job an awful lot easier when it comes to the crunch. Many a time I was able to write obituaries without looking at the files because you get to know a person so well. Many's the time I could approach a family when another newspaperman wouldn't have had a look in.

'I've picked the provost of Cullen. When the voting to elect the provost landed in a dead heat, they were looking for someone to draw a name from the hat and called me out from the press bench.

'I remember attending a public meeting at Portsoy when councillors were sitting on the stage in a platform party, ready to answer the community's concerns, but nobody turned up.

'I remember sending young John Bodie, who was just starting out as a reporter, to an event at a Banff hotel where they were going to pick that year's Banff Gala Lad and Lass. When he came back, I asked him who'd been picked and he said: "Well, the Gala Lad's me."

'I've chaperoned a German pilot who had returned to Banffshire to see where he'd been shot down during the war. He remembered a big policeman arresting him, and it turned out to be Chief Constable Strath. I put the two of them in touch and the axes were buried over a glass of home-made wine.

'There was Lonely Tom, up in Marnoch, who wrote us a letter in the late 1950s saying he was looking for a wife and needed help. He sent it to the Press and Journal's City Editor in London, for some reason. Anyway, I wrote up the story and he got 17 replies.

'I remember one Tory candidate speaking to me in the office and telling me seriously that he was in favour of electric-shock treatment in prison cells. If that chat had been on the record, he'd have been sunk.

'I remember saying that Hamish Watt wouldn't become Banffshire's MP, and he did — and a very good constituency MP he was.

'I've seen a son heckling his father at a political meeting. I've seen a husband heckling his wife.

'I've had the Press and Journal's news values denounced from the pulpit because of the way we reported the takings at a kirk sale of work.

'I've had a colleague visit the home of a prisoner who had been allowed out from jail in London so that he could attend his mother's funeral at Portsoy. The family had answered all his questions courteously, thinking he was from social work, or something, I suppose.

'Near the end, when the prisoner asked: "Who are you again?" and my colleague repeated that he was from the P and J, he had to run from the house for his own safety.

'There was a car chase round Portsoy before he managed to shake them. What a state he was

LEFT
The agricultural show was the big event in the rural community's social calendar, although many have long since passed into history. Alford Show, 1965.

ABOVE
The most northerly mainland burgh in the circulation area is Thurso, pictured here in 1969.

UW 7935
26
KA 6866
25

LEFT
Kildrummy Castle Rally was — and still is — a highlight in the June social calendar in the North-east. This is journey's end in 1967.

ABOVE
Turriff, one of the two towns where Press and Journal penetration habitually broke 100%, meaning that some households bought more than one copy. This is Turra in 1971.

in when he arrived back to safety at our Banff office.

'I remember the hoax when a giant sturgeon was supposedly landed at Macduff.

'I remember the sheriff who had dealt with all the pleading cases and, when there was only me, the sheriff clerk and fiscal in court, took off his wig, put his feet up on the bench, lit a cigarette and began dispensing justice in the least formal manner Scots law will ever see.

'I remember being in Canada with Ian Hardie, one of the Press and Journal's photographers. We were wandering about in Edmonton when a voice behind us said: "Ee're fae Aiberdeen." It was a couple who had seen Ian take a picture at a wedding in King's College Chapel.

'All of that — that's why I enjoyed my time as a district-office man.

'I can honestly say I've never regretted my career, and I've never regretted not leaving Banff and looking for advancement elsewhere. I did have people come through from Broad Street occasionally and ask me if I'd consider a move to head office, but I always said no. Head office wouldn't have been for me.

'And nowadays, when I look through my old contacts book, it grieves me to note how many of the good folk of Banffshire who gave me great help are no longer with us.

'I must emphasise the debt we district-office people owed to contacts at all levels of society.

'I believed firmly in attending innumerable unimportant annual meetings of various clubs, groups and societies, solely to keep in touch with people who, one day, might have "something" for the P. and J.

'On the whole, if I had my chances over again, I'd do it exactly the same. I suppose that makes me one of the lucky few, doesn't it?'

CHAPTER VIII

New Horizons

RIDING on healthy profits, soaring circulation, increased advertising revenue and the benevolent ownership of Roy Thomson, expansion was the obvious course for Aberdeen Journals. The company had opened district offices in Buchan and at Banff, to complement those in Inverness and Elgin. Both had proved that large towns were able to sustain daily-paper offices provided that readers of those editions felt they were buying papers with news that was relevant to them.

Lord Thomson was delighted with the turnaround in his Aberdeen fortunes and bade Ken Peters deliver more of the same. As a result, staff waited eagerly to hear where the next district office would be opened. In-house gossip favoured Wick, Golspie, Fort William, Huntly, Inverurie, Stonehaven or Perth.

Plans for a new office certainly were afoot, but the scheme was much more dramatic than anything being mooted on the Broad Street grapevine.

'We were as successful as any newspaper company could have been,' said Ken Peters, managing director, 'and we were successful *despite* our offices in Broad Street, rather than because of them. Head-office staff were very fond of Broad Street and its traditions, I knew that, but anyone with eyes to see would have realised how much the Broad Street premises were holding us back. It was just a collection of rambling, shambling old buildings, with doors and corridors hacked out of brickwork, stone and wood.'

The very name of Aberdeen's street of ink was the most celebrated misnomer in the city. A narrower major street than Broad Street did not exist. It was little more than a traffic-choked slit off the eastern end of Union Street, linking Union Street and Gallowgate, whose tenements on either side were so close together that sunshine barely intruded. The narrowness of the street made it a funnel for what seemed to be every northerly gale blowing anywhere near Aberdeen, picked up by the Spital, accelerated by the Gallowgate and finally blasted down Broad Street to the Harbour.

On Broad Street itself, the Journals frontage amounted to little more than 45ft of pavement, behind which lay a labyrinth of corridors, halls, windowless rooms, rickety stairs, awkward landings, partitions and knocked-through walls where the floors on either side never quite met. It was the legacy of decades of piecemeal expansion and make-do-and-mend alterations.

'Firemasters and factory inspectors must have shuddered and looked the other way when they walked past,' said Ken. 'We were turning out two of Scotland's biggest and most successful newspapers in premises which had been old tenement flats, a bakery (complete with oven), a dancehall (which became our wireroom), a chemist's shop, an undertaker's parlour (complete with coffins when we took over) and a room with an Adam fireplace in it.'

LEFT
A derelict site between the housing estates of Mastrick and Summerhill was eventually earmarked as the new home for Aberdeen Journals. From groundbreaking to first printing took two years and one month.

and so frequent that the council made Broad Street a one-way street to try to ease difficulties, which was decidedly unpopular with city motorists and delivery drivers.

Difficulties in Broad Street were innumerable, and made ever worse as Jimmy Grant and Ken Peters pushed through an Editorial and Commercial plan which piled success upon success.

'We were finding it difficult to expand as we knew we had to if we were going to keep pace with demand for the papers and with new technology,' said Ken. 'Given circumstances like that, it was inevitable we would look for a solution. And given that we were looking for a solution, it was inevitable that the rumour mill would start.'

Among allegedly likely locations for a Journals flit were the Aberdeen University Students' Union building on the corner of Gallowgate and Upperkirkgate; the site which later became St Nicholas House, the 1960s tower block HQ of Aberdeen City Council, and, as third candidate, most of the building occupied by Jamieson and Carry, the Union Street jeweller.

But smart staff money believed that all these rumours were as fanciful now as they had been for the previous half-century, and that Aberdeen Journals could not

RIGHT:
A rare photograph of the legendary William Veitch in later years. After his retirement, he attended Journals' pensioners' parties regularly.

EMERGENCY EXIT

LEFT:
The final days of the cash office at Broad Street, 1969.

ABOVE:
Preparing for the last dispatch of newspapers printed in Aberdeen city centre.

contemplate shifting from its prime city-centre site, where courts, councils, police and the City Bar were all within a minute's walk. For a newspaper company to do anything but stay put in those circumstances was self-evidently daft.

'There *had* been a scheme to renovate our Broad Street HQ,' said Ken. 'We'd even gone as far as drawing up plans, but we realised that no matter how heavily we redeveloped ourselves, it would always be just a facelift. Yes, it would have improved the frontage and done something about the public parts of the building, but no matter how we juggled it, it was just a fact that the space we needed for better equipment and more-modern presses simply didn't exist.

'Anyway, we couldn't have carried on producing two daily newspapers in conditions which were cramped at best, as well as doing a wholesale renovation round about everyone at the same time. It just wasn't on.'

Someone on the board hatched a plan to buy the entire south side of the street behind Broad Street. Queen Street was a string of drab tenements and old shops which backed on to the rear boundary of the Journals. In many ways, it was an inspired plan, for it would

'When I went away and thought about it, it seemed like an impossible task to shift an entire newspaper-production operation — staff, presses, typesetting, foundry, phones, the lot — over one weekend without a hitch. Basically, we were aiming to finish printing the Green Final in Broad Street on the target Saturday, and begin producing the Monday Press and Journal at Mastrick less than 24 hours later.'

Building work began at the start of 1969 on what had once been a rose nursery owned by the world-famous Aberdeen firm Cocker's. When the Operation Mastrick team convened in September, the target weekend for the move — November 14/15, 1970 — was still 14 months away. The team knew that the project was so complicated that even 14 months would be embarrassingly short.

'I felt that by breaking down the problem into controllable segments and taking care of those, the overall project would be much more manageable,' said Bill Jamieson. 'I hadn't done anything like it before but, then, who had? How often do you shift an entire newspaper operation across a city? I wouldn't say it was frightening — challenging, yes — but there were seven of us on the Operation Mastrick team and we were all pulling together.'

LEFT:
A dramatic early-morning blaze in the heart of Aberdeen in 1970 reduced a social club in the Adelphi to ruins.

RIGHT:
One of the bulkiest single items of machinery, the stereo moulding press, is lowered gently for removal to Mastrick. One slip here would have caused months of production and printing problems.

The principal difficulty became clear at the team's first meeting. Time and deadlines conspire against newspapers every minute of every day. The greatest challenge for Operation Mastrick would be not the mere 14 months allotted to the project but the deadlines and schedules which would have to be reworked entirely to ensure that newspaper production, which works to precise minutes every day, could work just as efficiently before, during and after the most complex flitting in Scottish newspaper history.

The *before* was working smoothly already. The *after* offered scope to rewrite production and distribution schedules from the ground up in a way that Broad Street could not have entertained. The *during* would be the greatest challenge.

The team's principal task once the likely difficulties had been set down on paper was to plan for printing during the transition. Installing a printing press and bedding it down to run smoothly takes at least six months, and the flit would involve moving not one full-sized newspaper press but two.

The way forward was dual printing — producing newspapers at Mastrick and at Broad Street for an eight-month transition. It was an inordinately complex logistical challenge that,

even now, three decades on, draws admiration from all who study the Operation Mastrick master plan.

The team members knew that they would have to arrange dismantling of one of the three Broad Street presses and reassembly at Mastrick in the early spring of 1970.

Once that was running smoothly and producing papers, the second major Broad Street press would be dismantled and reassembled at the new site, leaving only 'the pivot press', an old machine that was about to be retired, as Broad Street's last working press.

'Once the rebuilt first press was running smoothly, we began a courier service taking flongs [papermaché-like impressions of complete composed pages which were then used to cast metal printing plates for the presses] from Broad Street to Mastrick,' said Bill Jamieson.

'While we were doing that, the Circulation people were looking at the new logistics of getting papers out to the circulation area from an industrial estate on the edge of the city instead of a site bang in the centre.

'At the same time, we were bussing groups of staff up to the new building so they could see round and get an idea of the scale of the place and where they would be fitting in and working. On reflection, that was when we were at the peak of planning and activity. That was the most stressful time of the whole project.'

There is a story, perhaps apocryphal, of one group of staff being shown a large-scale model of the new premises, with each department marked so that staff could find their place. The architects, engineers and project managers were proud of the detail of their work, certain that they had covered every angle, down to number of desks, waste-paper bins and positions for coat-stands.

When the architects asked for questions, there was a heavy silence until they noticed one man studying the model more intensely than the others. They watched as he peered into corners, studied the two floors, stood back for an overall view, then peered inside again. His name was Albert Annand.

'Is this finished?' he inquired eventually, while intrigued colleagues looked on.

'Yes,' said one of the architects. 'This is exactly as it will be.'

'I dinna think so.'

'Y-yes. This is a scale model.'

'Bit this is nae the finished article, tak it fae me.'

'Why's that?'

'Because ye've designed a newspaper office withoot a wire room.'

According to legend, the first plans went as far as scale-model demonstration without providing any means of getting national and international stories into the building and into the two papers.

'MOVING the second press was a bit easier than the first,' said Bill Jamieson; 'we knew where the likely pitfalls would be and, if I remember, it went relatively smoothly and we were able to concentrate on other things.

'When the final weekend drew closer for most of the staff to shift, we had them crate up everything in colour-coded boxes so that the removers could instal the items in the right rooms at Mastrick at the first attempt.

'Of course, we still had other plant and machinery to shift even after the two rebuilt presses were working at Mastrick. There were Linotype and Klischograph machines that we couldn't shift until the last possible moment, and that was a bit nerve-racking.'

The police were exceptionally

LEFT:
A last look at the old office. Ken Peters (left) and Lord Thomson stand back after turning the key for the last time . . .

RIGHT:
. . .and are joined at the new headquarters by Aberdeen Lord Provost James Lamond (left) and Scottish Secretary Gordon Campbell (third left).

co-operative on the target Saturday night. After the last Green Final had finished running (and a spirited band of staff had begun doing the rounds of city-centre hostelries with a mock coffin to lament the passing of a piece of Aberdeen history), the constabulary closed three streets in the city centre while Journals personnel and haulage firms craned out the last of the Linotypes through a hole knocked in the Broad Street wall and put them on lorries.

The only hitch befell the trucks at the top of Westburn Road, where the hill from the city centre peaks at North Anderson Drive. A snap November frost — the only night frost of that autumn, as bad luck would have it — had made the top of the Westburn Road treacherously icy.

By the time the trucks had laboured up the long hill, they had no momentum to power over the ice and came lumbering to a halt. However desperately the drivers tried, their lorries' wheels would not grip and vital heavy machinery was stranded half a mile from its new home.

'We had to call out the council to come with grit,' said Bill. 'Considering the time of night, they were very quick and cheerful about it.'

The following day, work began on the Press and Journal of Monday, November 16, 1970. When the paper appeared, few readers knew the difference in the product or had any idea of the work, pressure and historical shift of the previous weekend.

It was the biggest compliment the Operation Mastrick team could have had.

'It wouldn't be right to say that we modernised by moving to Mastrick,' said Bill. 'We were still doing papers from hot-metal and we used Linotypes, but there is no question that moving to the Lang Stracht streamlined the operation; gave us a chance to rethink the whole process of producing newspapers, and gave us room to move. Anyway, I don't remember many complaints about the way the transfer was done or the result. To the public, it was more or less a non-event.

'One thing I do recall clearly was Ken Peters insisting very early on that the new building wasn't to be just another concrete monolith on an industrial estate, which most factories being built in the late Sixties were. Ken was very strong on history and heritage and that's why the surround at the main public entrance on the Lang Stracht HQ is in granite. I daren't think what it cost, but Ken felt it was an important gesture to the area.'

Lord Thomson attended the formal opening just before Christmas. Before he arrived at the Lang Stracht for the first time, he asked to be taken to see the now quiet and derelict shell of Broad Street. He and Ken Peters stood alone outside and stared at the locked building, silent after almost 80 years of 24-hour activity.

'He didn't say much,' said Ken. 'He just stood there in his black Crombie coat and homburg taking in everything. Then he turned to me and said: "Did you guys really turn out two daily newspapers from here?'

NOT everyone was happy with the move from Broad Street, even if all of them did recognise the difficulties imposed by the old place. Unanimously, journalists felt the shift was counter-productive. Moving a newspaper operation from the heart of city, where news is at its most concentrated and contacts are easiest to collar, to an industrial estate three miles out on the edge at the top of a wind-blasted hill would make gathering news many times more difficult, they said (and still say).

Most of all, the intense professional affection for Broad Street, despite all its limitations, made the final shift probably the greatest wrench of several hundred careers. Old hands still

The

LEFT:
A crowd gathers to watch the formal opening inside the new building. Gordon Campbell, now Lord Campbell of Croy, conducted the ceremony in part of the machine room where a second press had yet to be assembled.

ABOVE:
The VIP dinner to celebrate the opening. Lord Thomson looks remarkably glum for a tycoon.

look wistful when they talk of their apprentice years at the heart of the city.

'The Broad Street building was an absolute rabbit warren,' said Ethel Simpson, Scotland's first trained female journalist. 'But I loved it. It was special to me. It was where I started. It was where I got my chance to be a reporter. And, when you think of it, what a history went through that place. Some people worked their whole lives in that building and thought little or nothing of it. We all knew it was dilapidated, but we just all mucked in.

'I remember Lord and Lady Kemsley coming round some time after the war on a tour of the Kemsley group and being amazed by Broad Street. I remember him just looking at us and looking at the surroundings and saying that he would do his best about our conditions. I suppose he kept his word as much as he could.'

'A real newspaper place,' said Jimmy Lees, later Evening Express news editor. 'The stories of Broad Street are the stuff of legend in the trade. It was a crossroads for all the news and gossip and tittle-tattle in the North-east. As journalists we couldn't have been better placed.

'I still laugh at a conversation that followed someone pleading not guilty at the police court just round the corner. A JP or some such had listened to the Not Guilty plea then he had leaned imperiously across the bench and stared at the accused.

'Not guilty? Fit div ye mean Not Guilty? It'll be a' the worse for ye noo.'

'Another famous Broad Street story that did the rounds for years involved the Press and Journal farming editor, Alex Munro, attending Keith Show or Turriff Show and getting a bottle of beer from the secretary's tent. A few minutes later, there was a message over the Tannoy:

McKAY'S
CAUTION
DEMOLITION
IN PROGRESS

‘ “Wid Alex Munro fae the P. and J .come back til the secketry’s tint? Ye’re awa wi wir opener.”

‘Then there was the reporter who was doing journalism to finance his way through studies for the ministry. One Sunday, towards the end of his degree, he was due to take a church service for the first time and he was a wee bit keyed up about it.

‘When the Monday came, we asked him how the service had gone. We were never really sure if he was better suited to journalism or the clergy after that, because he said: “Weel, the prayers wis a bittie difficult, bit the sermon wis a bliddy caker.”

‘Or there was our network of correspondents. There were so many of them after Jimmy Grant’s rapid expansion in the Sixties that it was sometimes difficult to keep track of them all. One reporter phoned the home of an occasional corr for a briefing on some story or other that had happened in that village.

‘ “I’m sorry, he’s nae available,” said a voice.

‘ “I see,” said the reporter. “Will he be away long?”

‘ “I wid say so,” said the voice. “He dee’d twa year back.”

‘All in all, there must have been 14 or 15 reporters in Broad Street in the Fifties and Sixties. We worked for both papers in those days, shifting back and forth from one to the other. It was the late Sixties or early Seventies before the papers were split for good and P and J staff and EE staff were assigned full-time to one paper only. It made for more rivalry, but it was always good-natured rivalry.

‘As for Mastrick — ach — it was different completely, not like a newspaper office at all. It was open-plan. It was like a barn and the phones didn’t work and a lot of us felt that the staff didn’t really get any say in what department went where and what we really needed to do our jobs.’

‘There was great camaraderie at Broad Street,’ said Gordon Forbes. ‘I wouldn’t say it was a laugh a minute, but there was certainly a lot of laughing.

‘How could there not be camaraderie when you were working with subs like Bob Johnston, from Buckie?

‘Bob was the one who sorted out the 4am weather forecast for the last edition. He would walk across to the window, open it, stick out his hand and say: “Rainin.”

‘Bob also wrote the Donovan Smith column and sometimes, when we were four or five lines short on a page and we were tight against edition time, Bob would fill out the short leg with one-par stories about the latest exploits of the Italian opera diva Maria Ponjavi, or the retired World War II flying ace Günther Prieg.’

Neither Maria nor Günther existed outside Bob’s imagination, but through the Fifties, Sixties and early Seventies, Press and Journal readers were able to follow the careers of both in regular series of four- and five-line filler shorts.

Maria Ponjavi might be giving a recital in Amsterdam; or have been made a holder of the Legion d’Honneur after a cultural tour of Mauritius, or be taking a masterclass for a group of penniless Verdi enthusiasts in the Empire Opera House, Ulan Bator.

Günther was even more colourful, once buzzing the Empire State Building demanding better pension rights for retired Luftwaffe aces, and gatecrashing a state banquet of the Danish Royal Family to apologise for bombing one of their summer palaces after he had taken a wrong turning at Hamburg in 1942.

On one occasion, Günther and Maria are rumoured to have met, although no traceable record appears to exist of this encounter, another product of one of the most fertile, imaginative and witty minds to have been on the Press and Journal staff.

‘I don’t know if the chief sub, Bill

FAR LEFT:
Broad Street HQ died in the summer of 1973 as demolition teams moved in. For many staff with fond memories of the old office, her three-year dereliction was almost painful to witness.

McDonald, knew that Maria and Günther were pure fiction,' said Gordon Forbes, 'but I'm damned sure Jimmy Grant did and, even though he was Editor, Granter would just have had a wee laugh up his sleeve because he knew it wasn't doing any harm. It's that kind of humour and spirit that you don't get in newspapers nowadays. You wouldn't get away with it.'

'Bob was also possessed of a cartoonist's skill,' said Ron Knox, later assistant editor. 'He could capture a moment or reduce pomposity to ashes in a few devastating strokes. You knew you'd arrived when you stumbled across your caricature under Bob's blotter. Sometimes it was better not to look.

'But when the work was done in Broad Street, there always seemed to be time to relax at the end of the shift. There was time for a game of cards, off down to the fish market café at 4am for tea and bacon sandwiches, then off to bed. No wonder some of us had chronic weight problems.'

'The camaraderie of Broad Street was something I never experienced again,' said Pearl Murray. 'There was a notable lack of backstabbing in that place. Everyone appeared to be compatible, and enjoyed their work and each other's company, and I'm sure that it shone through in the finished products.

'I can tell you exactly how old-fashioned the place was: when I joined, the newsroom still had a coal fire, and there were no phones on desks; we had two phone booths if we needed to call anyone or take down copy.

'I never really adjusted to the open-plan of Mastrick. A writer needs smaller, quieter space and time to think. Open-plan offices can't give us that. I never felt that we were really the same family in Mastrick. The best thing about the transfer was that we retained Jimmy Grant as Editor.

'Mr Grant was the kind of man who could meet kings and commoners and treat them just the same. He never lost the common touch and staff respected him for that. His was a grand mind in a fair man.'

'There's still a feeling of unity among people who worked in Broad Street,' said Peter Watson, Editor from 1975 to 1986. 'It was almost like being in a military

RIGHT:
The Queen Mother paid the Lang Stracht a visit in 1972. Here, she watches a hot-metal page being assembled by compositor Bruce Booth.

unit. Broad Street colleagues were a very close-knit community. You had to be; the place had more people shoehorned into it than it could really stand.'

'It had warmth and caring, fun and laughter, a heart and a soul,' said Ethel Simpson. 'Reporters who came back on a visit from new jobs all over the world used to say their Broad Street days were the happiest of their career. I mind fine the day we were invited up to Mastrick in groups of twelve or fourteen, about three months before the flit, so we could see how the office looked and where we would be going.

'When we saw the big barn of an editorial hall, we were so depressed that we went back down to Broad Street in silence and across to the City Bar to drown our sorrows.'

Broad Street was demolished shortly after the Press and Journal and Evening Express decanted three miles up the hill. For a few months, the shell looked so forlorn and abandoned that many journalists could scarcely bear to pass by, so betrayed, suffering and reproachful did the building seem. When demolition came, many of the staff felt it was a mercy to a grand old lady.

Now, the space that churned history on to the streets of the North and North-east for almost a century is occupied by a modern extension to Aberdeen's grand old Town House. It is an office complex on stilts, clad almost entirely with small white ceramic tiles, thus ensuring that it earned its nickname in Aberdeen as the most lavish public toilet in Scotland.

The spirit of Broad Street lives on, however. Almost three decades later, mail arrives at the Lang Stracht from all corners of the globe, addressed to:

Press and Journal,
20 Broad Street,
Aberdeen
Scotland

And the old hands allow themselves a wee smile and a wallow in warm memories.

THE pressures of newspaper production don't allow for navel-gazing and contemplation. Any disgruntlement in the move to the Lang Stracht had to be forgotten quickly as a succession of running news stories broke, including some of the biggest of the latter half of the century.

The longest-running is running yet and brought wholesale change to life and work throughout the northern half of Scotland, yet when the Press and Journal broke the story in April, 1963, it earned first hoots of derision throughout the staff, then customary northern scepticism among the great majority of readers.

THE DON'S ARE THE GREATEST.
WINNERS OF
EUROPEAN CUP WINNERS CUP 1983
ALSO SCOTTISH CUP WINNERS 1983
Northern
SCOTTISH
POLICE
GCS
245

industry in which time was master. After long and frequently difficult negotiations, journalists' and advertising salespeople's typewriters were taken away and replaced with a dedicated newspaper word-processing network. Caseroom staff were offered voluntary-redundancy packages.

There was a deal of resentment at the pace of this forced change, and even more resistance, but once a new-technology wage deal and conditions package were concluded and the system installed, it took less than a month for advertising staff and journalists to marvel at how they had ever managed to put out newspapers using paper and typewriter.

The new system had its stiffest test in July, 1988. The tragedy of Piper Alpha still haunts many Scots journalists. Almost 170 men died when one of the North Sea's oil-production platforms exploded in a fireball.

The world's press descended on Aberdeen to cover a story which the industry and Scotland had hoped would never happen. Being the daily-newspaper office, the Lang Stracht became an ad hoc base for foreign journalists and more than 50 of them — and two dozen different languages — filled the building as they worked in whatever odd corners they could find and queued to use

Press and Journal

THE FAMOUS GROUSE

SPECIAL LATE ABERDEEN EDITION

241st Year THURSDAY JULY 7 1988 No. 41,587 24p

193 OILMEN FEARED DEAD

5a.m.

Piper Alpha platform blown apart

By DAVID STEELE and IAIN LUNDY

Inside story

Ship rams rocks

Graduation stories, pictures — PAGES 9, 10 and 11

Act fast, Newton demands

Travel firm fail

On other pages:

Sobbing woman greets survivor

By DAVID STEELE

RIG BLAST LATEST

Serious accidents part of life on rigs

WEATHERGUIDE

No stranger to accidents . . .

Advice to pilots

FAR LEFT:
The joy of Aberdeen FC fans as the Dons return from Sweden after winning one of Europe's greatest club trophies.

LEFT:
The tragedy of one of the most heart-rending stories the Press and Journal has covered.

phones, Telexes, faxes, picture wires and computer links.

In newspaper terms, it's a tribute to the trade that facilities were offered so readily to so many when the Press and Journal's own production demands were so complex, and the edition structure timed so tightly.

Staff journalists who were on holiday or having a day off turned up to offer their colleagues help on what they knew would be the busiest news day of their careers. Many of the volunteers tackled the humbler, but essential, diary-based stories of the day while the duty staff in Aberdeen, Inverness, Elgin and Buchan, and correspondents everywhere from Shetland to Perth pulled together to cover one of the most harrowing stories of the century.

The Press and Journal has always handled big-breaking stories smoothly, almost as if a plan of campaign existed, but the trick on a heavy news day is not in covering the big story; it's in making sure that all the lesser tales are still told with the same punch and accuracy.

Jim Kinnaird was duty night editor when the story broke. A customarily quiet night legalling stories and writing newsbills suddenly reared up and raged about him, presenting coverage difficulties few other Editorial executives have had to face. Jim

Press and Journal

241st Year | THURSDAY DECEMBER 22 1988 24p | No. 41,731

GOOD MORNING ABERDEEN

CRISIS SOLVED! Gift Vouchers from NOVA

Wreckage destroys 40 houses

'It was raining fire, liquid fire . . .'

Plane was 'loaded with Xmas presents'

FIREBALL!

Jumbo crash toll put at 280

Grampian teams on full alert

WEATHER

CONTENTS

EMERGENCY numbers for people worried about relatives are: 01 897 6333; 01 750 9464; 01 750 9506; 01 750 9508; 01 750 9548. Pan Am's emergency number in the US is 0101 212 880 1234.

Left like a war zone

Impact 15 miles from N-plant

Aberdeen units made offer of help

'Shocked' Queen being kept informed

☐ MORE PLANE DISASTER NEWS ON PAGES 6 AND 7 ☐

Messages. A.C. YULE EMERGENCY GLAZING. A FREE MESSAGE BOARD! WHEN YOU CALL FOR YOUR EMERGENCY GLAZING. THE EMERGENCY GLAZING NUMBER. 890000 FOR YOUR 24 HOUR SERVICE A.C. YULE

Helen Hunter. 100 ROSEMOUNT PLACE ABERDEEN. QUALITY FASHION SALE Today 9.30. VERY SPECIAL SAVINGS!

LEFT:
Press and Journal news teams covered the Lockerbie disaster on the spot.

RIGHT:
Regular access to the nation's decision-makers is a feature of Press and Journal news and political coverage. Features writer Lynn Montgomery quizzed Prime Minister Margaret Thatcher at length in 1990.

masterminded the 5am special edition which broke the appalling news.

It remains an immense tribute to Jim, to Eric Stevenson and his newsroom team, Jimmy Urquhart and his sub-editing team, Editor Harry Roulston and the many production departments who handled the extraordinary 24-hour demands, pressures and emotion of the Piper Alpha story with no complaint and great skill that the resulting newspapers were praised even by those who had lost loved ones so tragically; by foreign journalists who could scarcely comprehend how order, accuracy and respectful coverage had come from such chaos, and by ordinary readers who wrote some of the most moving Letters to the Editor that the features department had handled.

Deservedly, the Press and Journal Piper Alpha team members were named Journalists of the Year in the 1988 Press Awards.

Co-operation and professionalism were at their height that week in July, 1988.

No one knew that darker clouds were looming.

ALL large companies and large unions suffer their share of industrial disputes, especially in newspaper publishing. The many different newspaper trades have been represented by as many different unions almost since the founding of the union movement in Scotland in 1897. Such a broad church has always resulted in several different sets of annual negotiations, several different types of industrial grievance, and several potential battlegrounds.

From the early 1920s, a succession of minor management-union spats over wages, hours and conditions at the Daily Journal and the Free Press were resolved usually without stopping publication.

Ironically, when an industrial dispute did cripple publication of the Press and Journal, management and staff relations had rarely been better. The General Strike was called in May, 1926, after efforts to solve a national miners' dispute had failed. Every trades unionist in Britain, including compositors and journalists, was required to leave work to show solidarity with brother miners.

The best that Aberdeen Newspapers could put out for the first week of the General Strike were single A4 sheets run off on a duplicator. There was space for only two or three lines each to cover national and regional stories, as well as strike news, but they still cost 1d. Only six of these strike issues were published and very few examples survive.

Ultimately, the General Strike was declared illegal and collapsed in10 days. Aberdeen Newspapers management introduced a strict no-union policy and sent messages to all striking staff to offer reinstatement, but only if the strikers relinquished union membership. All but a handful accepted the terms, effectively banishing unions from Broad Street for two and a half years. Unions did not reappear until they were invited back and encouraged by the Berry Brothers' new management in 1928.

George Fraser, then a 30-year-old sub-editor at Broad Street, remains convinced that the fundamental flaw in General Strike tactics was that the organisers did not give newspaper staff special dispensation to work on. 'By calling out newspaper workers,' he said, 'the organisers left themselves with no means of getting their point across to the public, and that was their undoing. The strike was doomed almost from the start.

'As for me, I felt strongly that I had no quarrel with my employer and I remained at my post. I suppose I became a bosses' man, if you want to put it that way, but we had no compositors, anyway, so no matter how many journalists worked, we couldn't get proper papers out. Some of the office girls tried to work the Linotype machines, but they made a right mess of it, and that was why we had to resort to the single sheets off the Roneo.

'I'll always remember as the strike was beginning to crumble, that the head of the comps, a Boer War veteran, walked into the caseroom and glared around him. We all looked at him, then he hauled off his jacket and marched up to his post. "Get oot o ma sicht," he told a lassie sitting at his Linotype seat. "Ye're bladdin ma machine." And he set about working again.'

BILL FORSYTH worked in Aberdeen Journals senior management in the Sixties, Seventies and early Eighties, retiring in 1982 as assistant managing director. 'We had many disputes and several stoppages,' he said, ' but there was never real acrimony in the negotiations. There was always give and take, and we'd finish on a handshake in the end and everyone would go back as before. If you like, there was an understanding on both sides as to how far you could push a point.

'I remember a row blowing up over one of our Inverness van-drivers giving people lifts in his van, which is against company policy. The problem was that he hadn't stopped at giving lifts; he had begun charging for them. Then he'd been a wee bit more ambitious still and he'd started picking up paying passengers at bus stops.

'Naturally, Highland Omnibuses wrote to complain and we had to act. We called a meeting with the transport union in the boardroom and explained that the next driver caught doing it would be sacked.

'It became very tense — newspaper unions were very, very powerful in those days — and the father of the transport chapel [van drivers' shop steward] put forward a very strong case to the effect that, often, it actually helped the company if van-drivers offered certain people lifts. It was good PR.

' "What about the country bobby who gives us tipoffs?" he said. "What about the wife of the farmer who gets out his tractor and hauls us out of drifts in the

RIGHT
Inverness railway bridge collapses in the floods of February, 1989. The tracks gave way a few minutes after this picture was taken.

winter? You can't just drive past these people if you spot them in the middle of nowhere in the pouring rain."

'They were reasonable points, so I considered this for a while, then I leaned across and repeated very firmly: "There - are - *no* - passengers."

'And then I winked.

'He understood what I meant and he stood up. We shook hands. We'd both made our points. We were both happy with the line we'd drawn, and there was no walkout.'

THE ROAD to harmonious industrial relations in all newspaper companies became rockier from the mid-1980s. Technology and computerisation were at the root of it. Managements anxious to reduce the industry's traditionally high costs, and unions equally determined to protect their members and jobs, began a series of complex and testing negotiations. Virtually every newspaper company in Britain had regular walkouts as management and unions drew the lines that suited them best. The passion was understandable; ultimately, the results of these negotiations would change the operation of British newspaper companies for good.

Production departments were the first to experience wholesale change. From the early 1980s, computerisation began sweeping through the pre-press part of the industry, particularly in caserooms, where type was set and pages assembled. Work done at one time by a dozen caseroom men could now be done by four. Management and production unions negotiated new-technology payments and redundancy packages. The company asked for 38 voluntary redundancies and received 76 applications.

Matters culminated in 1986 with a long sequence of negotiations in which union after union presented wage claims between 15% and 20% and refused further redundancies.

This particular round made Aberdeen boardroom life difficult and exasperating; in 1986, the oil price had collapsed; the economy of the northern half of Scotland had stagnated within weeks, and Aberdeen Journals was staring at a £2million loss of revenue.

Managing director Alan Scott called a meeting of Scottish newspaper-union leaders and explained the grave commercial position. 'They made sympathetic noises,' said former Press and Journal Editor Harry Roulston, 'but they pressed ahead with their demands, anyway.'

Ultimately, these multiple disputes were settled, but the experience had steeled Alan Scott to ensure that Aberdeen Journals 'would not be held to ransom again'. He called a series of meetings with senior management and drew up plans for emergency newspaper production to cover future strikes.

Middle management was trained in how to use the presses; how to operate the dispatch machines, how to set type on computer, how to assemble pages and how to make printing plates. Many of these managers had come through the trades, in any case, so the training programme was remarkably quick.

Alan Scott was now confident that middle managers could cope with setting type, making plates, running the presses, baling the papers and distributing them, but the power of the National Union of Journalists — all but a handful of the 180 journalists at Aberdeen Journals were NUJ members — meant that writing and assembling the words and pictures would be almost impossible if the only journalists left at their desks were the two Editors, working solo for their respective papers.

'We had agreements with the production unions that their departments' middle managers were regarded as management and would stay in post during disputes,' said Alan Scott, 'and it seemed illogical to me that the NUJ regarded Editorial department heads — features editors, sports editors, picture editors, news editors, and so on — as union members first and managers second.

'That led to the ridiculous situation of a relatively junior member of staff, if he happened to be a union official, being able to order his boss to leave his desk. It was nonsense. None of the other unions in the place put up with that. I can't think of another industry which would have tolerated it, so it was natural that we wanted everyone on the same footing.'

The 32 editorial managers and specialists were asked to accept that they were managers first, union members second, and were invited to sign personal contracts on that basis. Almost half agreed. The others, concerned by this unexpected lurch in union-management relations, took the proposal to the Editorial chapel [NUJ Aberdeen Journals branch]. The chapel called in the national union.

Both sides knew that the key to producing or stopping the newspapers in future lay with the allegiance of editorial managers and specialists. As a result, these few dozen people were caught at the core of what was to become the most acrimonious dispute in Scottish newspaper history.

Harry Conroy was general secretary of the NUJ and a familiar face in newspaper offices throughout the country. 'I never liked disputes,' he said, 'but this one alarmed me because the Aberdeen papers were part of the Thomson Organisation, and I had already been involved in a storm at the Scotsman, also a Thomson paper, when their managing director had taken me to one side and said, rather chillingly: "Harry, I should tell you that if your members go out, I'm under instructions to destroy the union."

'So I travelled to Aberdeen sure in my mind that this personal-contracts situation was part of some grander Thomson plan.'

Alan Scott invited at least one other union leader to the meeting with Harry Conroy. There, the managing director explained his views on where the allegiances of editorial managers should lie and invited the third man to confirm that every other newspaper union regarded middle managers as managers.

'He agreed. I remember him turning to Harry and saying very plainly that the NUJ was alone among the six unions in the industry in not accepting that middle managers were managers first and union members second, but Harry refused to accept it.'

NUJ general secretary Harry Conroy led striking journalists through a three-week dispute in the autumn of 1989 and reached a settlement. He had to handle a second dispute, lasting for more than a year, a few weeks later.

On August 18, 1989, a furious meeting of the Aberdeen journalists' chapel regarded personal contracts as an affront to union principles and the first stage of Aberdeen Journals derecognising the union. Of 180 journalists, more than 100 went on strike.

Shortly before journalists left the building on the Friday morning to attend the meeting which called the strike, an Evening Express reporter's last action was to delete her whole week's work from the computer system. She did it knowing that if, as seemed inevitable, a strike was called, the whole of Saturday's Evening Express would be in jeopardy.

The strike was called. Journalists who remained at their posts worked well beyond their hours to make up the shortfall caused by the reporter's deletion of her work and the Saturday issue appeared as normal.

Meanwhile, the company sent letters to all journalists assuring them that the NUJ was still recognised and could negotiate for all journalists who had not signed individual contracts.

'We were out for three weeks,' said Harry Conroy. 'Quite frankly, the dispute was crippling the union with the compensation payments we had to make, so no one was more relieved than me when we settled. I still wouldn't regard it as a win for the union, but we settled, and at least we still had a union.

'The settlement came in the most bizarre circumstances. We met on neutral ground — a minister's house at Cults — where we hammered out the details. I took the proposals back to the chapel and persuaded them to accept the deal. Let's say that they were far from happy, but they went back grudgingly.'

Shortly before the strikers returned to work, Alan Scott called a meeting of working journalists in the boardroom at the Lang Stracht to explain the terms of the settlement. As they made to leave, he stopped them. 'I want to make it clear,' he said, 'that there is to be no victimisation of the people who return. Things will be difficult for a few days, because this has been a very nasty situation for both sides, and I don't want this to flare up again.'

Following the return to work, the Evening Express reporter who had deleted her work was called to see her editor and was asked to account for herself.

In normal circumstances, her behaviour would have meant summary dismissal and would not have been defended by her union.

But the circumstances were far from normal, as the EE editor recognised. The company faced a profound industrial-relations dilemma at an ultra-sensitive time. Those journalists who had worked through the dispute expected a sacking for industrial sabotage, while those who had been on strike were alert for any sign of victimisation, specifically forbidden by the Cults agreement. The EE editor decided to take time to consider every aspect.

Before he had given his decision on what action, if any, he would take against the reporter, the union cried victimisation and convened a chapel meeting. Within hours, they were on strike for the second time in three weeks. Days later, after two ultimata, they were sacked.

THE chapel began a model public-relations campaign, persuading many Scottish local authorities to boycott the company by refusing to co-operate with working journalists and cancelling advertising contracts. MPs were primed to make public and Commons statements. With personal contacts throughout the media, the strike committee was able to present the union case with clarity and speed. The company, meanwhile, issued only written statements, with considerably less effect.

Within hours, the image of the dispute in the Scottish public mind was one of rogue employer and exploited staff. Being largely fair-minded, Scots responded and circulation began to slide downwards.

'It was an excellent campaign,' said Alan Scott. 'I have to give them that. It was admirable in its speed and the image it got across. I'd have been disappointed in them with anything less; we'd trained them, after all.

'But there were almost as many journalists vehemently opposed to the dispute — seventy-four — as there were in favour — a hundred and six. It was telling that none of the other newspaper unions was prepared to support them, despite many attempts at persuasion, and when the local authorities began boycotting us, saying they were protecting workers, they were forgetting and infuriating the six hundred staff still in the building.'

Working staff were certainly infuriated, particularly when the first boycotting authority, Gordon District Council, introduced its bans only on the strength of chapel claims.

When working journalists, incandescent with rage, called the council to ask why no one had sought a company view so that the council might at least have reached a balanced decision, a spokesman for the ruling Liberal Democrats said that councillors had no need to; 'Aberdeen Journals' policy of worker-exploitation' was 'well-known'.

But the dispute had not split on the simplistic lines that councillors, politicians and the public imagined. Several of those on the picket lines were ardent free-market Tories, and many of those determined to work were former and current union officials. Anger and indignation were equally vehement on both sides of the picket lines.

The journalist most respected by both sides during the dispute, then deputy editor Duncan MacRae, kept close counsel. He offered no public opinions and few private ones, crossing picket lines quietly to go to work. When a non-journalist member of staff asked in the depths of the dispute what Duncan thought of events, he replied: 'In nearly forty years in the trade, I've not known this. Those people out there are my colleagues.'

Now retired in Inverness, Duncan puts the most unhappy episode in Press and Journal history into clearer perspective.

'I was very fortunate through the dispute,' he said. 'I was in the union but, seeing as I was deputy editor, I was not part of the strike. I was relieved from a lot of the problems. I just did my job, but the whole atmosphere between both sides was falling apart.

'I could see why Alan Scott had taken the view he had. It was hopeless trying to cope with people after the first dispute. They were clearly of a mood that they would strike whenever it suited them.

'Nobody in their right mind sets out to get rid of three-quarters of the journalists at a major daily paper, but the fact remains that there were people on the picket lines that any paper would have been glad to get rid of. The sadness was that, in the process, we lost several very fine journalists.

'Some days, the working staff were very, very low. Some days, it was better. Non-journalistic staff, who were not involved, were quite happy, but the reporters, photographers and feature-and sports writers took the brunt of it. They had to go in and out through the picket lines regularly, and the baying and shouting can't have been very pleasant.'

He reserves his greatest opprobrium for the boycotting councils. 'Frankly, most of them haven't a leg to stand on over their attitude during the strike. They made up their policies on the basis of rumour and conjecture. They were trotting out some very bizarre views — ridiculous views which demonstrated only their abject ignorance of newspapers and the real working conditions in Aberdeen Journals. They didn't know the first thing about the background, but they spoke up, anyway.

'But the people who lose most in these affairs are always the workers. A strike is an admission of total failure by everyone involved. I suspect that Harry Conroy and his pals would have done better for our striking colleagues if they had had a free hand, but there were darker NUJ hands at work behind the scenes.'

Harry Conroy was not involved in calling the second strike.

'The first dispute was justified,' he said. 'No one will tell me otherwise. The second — the one that lasted for nearly a year — was unwinnable. It was engineered behind my back when I was out of the country. If I had been informed, I would have tried to stop it.

'I had been visiting Norwegian journalists in Oslo for a few days at the end of September, 1989. I got back on the Sunday night and I got into my house and the phone rang. It was a union official from Aberdeen. "What do you think, then, Harry?" he said.

' "What do I think about what?"

' "We're out again."

'I nearly collapsed. I couldn't believe it, not after all the work we'd put into the first settlement. I told him: "We have a major problem.

' "No, no," he said. "We can win it."

'"Listen," I said. "The only way we can win is if they sack the managing director and they'll never do that. Why did the chapel come out?"

' "Victimisation."

' "And how do we prove that?"

The Aberdeen official then asked who would be handling the dispute for the NUJ.

Despite his reservations, Harry Conroy took the helm of the dispute for almost all its run, until his members voted him out of office. Now running his own public-relations company in Glasgow, his stormy union-leading days behind him, he feels his leadership was undermined by ambitious NUJ lieutenants in London who, he says, waited until he was out of the country to call the second strike which they knew he would have opposed.

'But I'm still angry that Aberdeen Journals broke a key clause in our Cults agreement,' he said. 'Under the terms of that agreement, Alan Scott was required to meet me to discuss any future disputes which were boiling up. He never did. He just let it happen. Once it did, his management refused to meet me.'

Alan Scott disagrees. 'I called

Bob Hughes, MP, who had taken a very even line through the dispute, and said:
"Look, Bob, I think they're going to go out again and there's nothing I can do to stop it." I told him I was faxing Harry Conroy at NUJ headquarters, which I did.'
The fax did not reach Harry Conroy.
Only his lieutenants were in NUJ HQ that day.
'I still think workers have a right to withdraw labour,' said Harry. 'And I still think that personal contracts are wrong, and that no management has the right to sack workers who are in official dispute. But the Aberdeen chapel was tactically wrong and the strikers got into a situation which I couldn't pull them out of. That's a very hard thing to say. But it's absolutely true.'
The dispute was settled in September, 1990. It had run for almost a year
'We're weaker now,' said Harry. 'If that second dispute had not happened, the union would not have gone £1million in debt, and I might still have been General Secretary. Britain might have a single, powerful media union for print workers, journalists and everyone involved in newspapers and broadcasting. As it was, the Aberdeen result was a watershed. We are now divided.'

Most of the Journals strikers were given a severance payment. Some returned to work.
'We were actually keen to get as many back as possible,' said Harry Roulston, then Editor. 'But a lot of them had abandoned the strike long before it ended to get jobs elsewhere. A few of the ones who were left were beyond the pale, but the others were good journalists and sound people. For our part, we bore no grudge.
'But we'd forgotten the mood of the people who had worked for the paper throughout. They were angry after twelve months of picket lines and councillors' hot air and arrogance. They told senior management very forcibly that they couldn't work with the real hotheads of the picket-lines, or the ones who had pulled the council strings, so we gave the staff who had worked the final say on whether or not those strikers who had applied for their old jobs were actually taken back.'
With normal service resumed, the company turned its attentions to rebuilding circulation, which had slid, in the Press and Journal's case, from 110,000 to around 90,000.
'We didn't need to do much to get the councils to lift their bans,' said Alan Scott. 'They were rescinded instantly, almost as if it was a relief. A lot of individual councillors were sorry they'd ever got involved, and I don't think many will make the mistake again of taking a public stance on an issue which didn't involve them, on which they were so poorly briefed, and which just dragged them deeper.'
Today, the 1989-90 dispute is largely forgotten inside and outside the trade. Most of the strikers work elsewhere in the British media. Many of the rest who manned the picket lines for the year now work side by side with those who stayed in and worked 16-hour days, and the acrimony of the bitterest dispute in Scottish newspaper history has faded. Relations are repaired to such a degree that it is hard to recall who stood on which side.

ABOVE
Skye Bridge nears completion in March, 1995.

RIGHT
More than 90,000 people packed Union Street, Aberdeen, in July, 1994, for the party to commemorate the 200th birthday of the street's planning.

GALLOPING
HORSES

Just some of several hundreds of staff based at head office in the Lang Stracht, Mastrick, Aberdeen

CHAPTER IX

Teamwork

The Press and Journal is more than just reporting. Of the 750 people who work at the 11 offices of Aberdeen Journals, only 170 are journalists. For a flavour of the many jobs which ensure that the paper appears each morning, here are the stories of 26 in various parts of the company

ADVERTISING

Lorraine Smith

I'D ALWAYS intended going to art college when I left Buckie High, but I had an independent streak and I saw an advert for advertising staff at the Press and Journal. My mother was in the background, furious. She was saying: 'Get off that phone!' I was only 17 and they preferred people of 20, but I told the truth and they took me on, anyway.

It was a two-week training programme. The first week was How to Sell and How to Help the Client. The second was the administration and the computer.

That was eight years ago and I've loved every minute.

A good sale can keep you floating all day. If you have a slack day, you just have to learn to switch off at five o'clock and start with a clean slate next morning.

I worked on the farming ads for quite a while; I think farmers

prefer speaking to a local voice. Some of my English colleagues couldn't make out the farmers at all, but I thought they were great.

The P and J will take ads for most things, but we won't do chatlines and the like.

We've turned down a lot of revenue by that policy, but a Press and Journal reader deserves better than that stuff.

ARTISTS

Jayne Anderson

SOMETIMES, I think other people in the building must find it odd. There they are, working away at all this computer technology and the whole place is in pandemonium with deadlines, and there I am, back to basics with watercolours or sketchpad, doing my doodles.

I'm one of the team that produces the graphics and freehand illustrations for the paper. I did graphic arts and illustration at college and it took seven months to find a job, but I'm really happy with what I found. I couldn't believe my luck, because when students show a portfolio, they're used to employers saying: 'That's smashing, but . . .'

I remember my first assignment: I had to design a graphic map showing all the golf courses in the P and J area. Sometimes, deadlines are a bit

tight, and I always think a job looks better given time, but you don't get time in newspapers.

They're very good about leaving me to my own devices, though, and I've especially enjoyed doing artwork for the Lifestyle page and the covers for some of the special supplements we do.

The great thing about my job is definitely the variety.

CANTEEN

Peggy Argo

I COULDN'T count the tins of beans I've opened in 18 years on the night shift, but it's a lot. Great big catering tins. My night crowd are famous for their beans. Beans on toast. Beans and chips. Beans, beans, beans. Anything with beans and they're happy. The funny thing is that there's hardly a tin opened for the day staff. They don't go for beans.

Things have improved, diet-wise, in my time. We're selling fruit and salads now. We never used to do anything like that, but there's more of a demand.

We've also got more vending machines, but we're selling fizzy drinks, as well, and we never used to do that when I started.

The canteen in those days wouldn't touch anything out of the ordinary. A glass of milk was healthy eating in those days.

The older ones still like a square meal, of course. The sub-editors like to sit down to something substantial, but the younger ones usually stick to soup. Maybe it's because soup's cheap, I don't know. Some of them have begun bringing in their own sandwiches.

I think some of my customers would like a few more old-fashioned meals like mince and tatties instead of pasta bakes,

but that's not for me to decide.

There used to be three of us on night shift, but now there's only one at a time. I work four nights and Shirley Graham works three.

It makes it a bit of a rush, because I cook to order as much as I can, and it's not easy to keep an eye on an omelette, gammon and whatever else, as well as selling plated meals, sorting out the vending machines and looking after the till all at once.

I finish at two in the morning. By the time I get home, I make a cup of coffee, haul on my dressing-gown and settle in front of the TV to watch an old film. I couldn't be bothered cooking.

CIRCULATION

Allister Shacklock

I REMEMBER once manning the P and J marquee at the Keith Show. It must have been in the mid-1970s because there was a big sugar shortage on and the stuff was like gold dust. Anyway, people started coming up to the tent waving copies of the paper and wanting to know where their free bag of sugar was. I didn't know anything about any free bag of sugar.

It turned out that the vendor going round the rings was shouting: 'Free bag of sugar with every Press and Journal!' He thought everyone would understand it was a joke. Most of them did. And we shifted a few papers that day.

Circulation is basically the department that makes sure the paper gets from the Lang Stracht to retail outlets all over the northern half of Scotland before they open. More than 60% of our print is home-delivered.

We've 11 editions and an area bigger than many European countries to cover, so it's not always that easy. By the time the paper drops through a reader's letterbox, there could have been sheer pandemonium going on to get it there.

We use our own vans for virtually all of it, and that makes

us unusual in modern publishing, but we also use planes, trains, buses, postbuses, taxis and milk floats. I believe that once, when the Buchan road was blocked by snow, we even hired a trawler to go up the coast and drop off at Peterhead and Fraserburgh. The P and J must get through.

The big change I've seen in 25 years is the upheaval in retail.

Before, we could choose our retailers. Now, we're obliged to supply to whoever asks, and that means superstores and filling stations.

That has made life difficult for the stand-alone newsagent and a lot have closed.

COMMERCIAL

Maureen Mackie

WE'RE one of the departments in the commercial side, handling the day-to-day money. We're the Cash Office. We process the advertising receipts, staff expenses, accounts for subscription copies and we process payments to freelance writers and photographers through a section known as Contributor Accounts.

I began at Broad Street in 1969. They started me as the office junior — a lot of firms did that with new staff in those days — and I would make the tea in the big urn in time for the teabreak at half-past ten and go out to Mitchell and Muil's for the rowies. As usual, when someone left or retired, everyone moved up a rung and a new junior came in. Now I'm Head Cashier.

There are only six of us in the department, but it runs like clockwork. I've a good team.

We've got about 300 regular contributors, for pictures and text. I'm not saying if I think they're overpaid or underpaid for what they do; we just process the payments that Editorial fix for whatever outside work they use in their pages.

Some freelances say our rates are poor, but they're probably comparing us with UK nationals

or Sunday supplements and the like. Most are happy.

The number of contributors has stayed pretty steady — about 300. There are the regulars in the features, news and sports pages, and there are a few one-offs that will stay on our books for a while but are never really accepted again, and there are agencies.

Once a freelance work appears, the payment begins to process through the system.

We prefer to pay by bank transfer because it's quicker than processing cheques and getting them signed and sent.

Payment takes four to eight weeks to reach the contributor.

COMPUTERS

Iain Tavendale

THERE'S been more change in newspapers in the last 20 years than there were in the previous 200, although you could probably say the same about many industries. It's thanks to computers.

I'm the Pre-press development Manager, which means that I look after the Editorial and Production computer systems and keep things ticking over.

You have to keep on top of developments in the industry, as well, and take advantage of new technologies when they become available.

The revolution started really with the Apple Macintosh computer. We started away back with one little machine as a sort of trial to see how it might lay out advertisements. It became clear pretty quickly that we'd stumbled on something big and that there were far wider implications than just ad make-up.

Now we have about 100 Macs and they're used for making up the Editorial pages, making up the advertisements and for the artists doing design and illustration work.

The Mac meant big economic benefits to this company in terms of saving time and effort and staffing costs. You could say that

99.9% of what people read and see in the Press and Journal will have gone through a Mac at least once.

Yes, we've had the occasional system crash, but not so much now. There was a time, when people weren't familiar with the system, that I'd be phoned at home quite regularly.

The problems are not usually spectacular. The worst is when a finished page is sent off through the computer system and doesn't emerge at the other end and you have to trace it back to find out where it's lurking.

Mind you, with deadlines, that can be pretty spectacular.

COPY-TAKERS

Helen Hepburn

THE night Aberdeen FC bought one of its Dutch players, someone in the P and J sports department asked a Dutch newspaper to send us a background story on him. The only problem was that the Dutch reporter who phoned it through couldn't speak English. I think we ended up with about three usable words.

Then there was the night that Jim Dolan, who was our chief football writer at the time, was phoning in a match report from a football ground when all the lights were switched off and he was locked in.

But it's not always like that. We're basically here to take stories across the phone from reporters out and about. We take copy from the correspondents, too. While they read it out, we're sitting at a computer terminal with headphones on, typing what they say.

Some are easier to make out than others, but you never lose the rag with them . . . well, maybe after you put the phone down, but never while they're on the line.

Technology has caught up with us. When I started in 1978, there were nine full-time and three part-time news telephonists and we all used typewriters. Now

we're computerised and more and more reporters use laptop computers when they're out and about, so we're down to three full-time and six part-time.

But I like the variety. In some ways, you're the first to hear the news as the reporters phone it through. It was like that with Piper Alpha and Lockerbie.

I did 17 years on nights. I did it so that I could look after my children through the day, and my husband could mind them at night. I didn't want strangers looking after my papooses.

It worked fine. Mind you, we didn't have any social life for nearly two decades.

DISPATCH

Steve Thomson

EVERYTHING used to be done by hand in Dispatch, but now it's computerised. Most is tracked, counted, stacked and tied by machinery. Most of the machinery is Swiss or Scandinavian.

Dispatch is the department between the press and the vans. We work closely with Production, Circulation and Distribution.

The first job of the night is to plan for that night's supply. We take the slips from Circulation and enter them in the computer. If a late story breaks and Editorial expects that more papers will sell, we're the people who make sure that newsagents' supplies are adjusted up to suit.

We print the labels for all the bundles, then we set up the Thorsted, a machine that wraps the individual copies for posting. We do the newsbills for the boards outside newsagents. The Night Editor writes them and we get them printed. We used to have to print them all out by hand but, with Apple Macintosh computers everywhere, that's a lot cleaner.

It's not often that our machinery breaks down. If ever there is a problem it might be a technical thing to do with the press. When

that happens the Dispatch man in charge has to work out how to get round it and the staff on shift really put their backs into it.

We ask if we should put the previous edition to the next circulation area, say the North-east edition to Gordon; call out extra vans, or ask Editorial to telescope the next two editions together to counter the lateness.

When the last edition's away, we're still not finished; there's a lot more printing of other things through the night. Every Saturday, the Journals prints the News of the World on contract.

And there'll be a lot more business like that.

DRIVERS

Brian Walker

I SUPPOSE there was a time when anyone would be driving round Aberdeen and if they saw a P and J van in their mirror they would pull over just to get out of the road. Us and the posties; we had reputations for hammering on to meet the deadlines.

It's not the same nowadays. The shift patterns for the day staff have changed so there's not the same pressure to cut time on the first run to get an easy second run. And we've all been on a Drive and Survive course.

The courses fairly worked. I was hearing the other day that the firm's accident rate is well down. We're able to do the deliveries as quickly, but more safely.

When you think of the number of miles that the vans do in a year, the accident rate is next to nothing, really.

There are 39 drivers on the staff, between day shift for the Evening Express and night shift for the P and J. If I start at 11.30 at night, we'll load up the vans with the first edition for the Highlands. Three vans will go to the Highlands. There'll be a Transit for Inverness town itself and for delivering to John Menzies wholesalers. A big box van meets the company drivers who are based at Inverness and

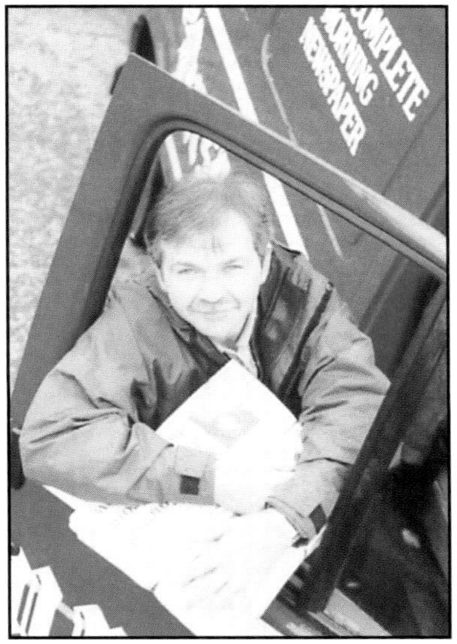

transfer the papers into their vans for going round the Highlands. Then a later van will go up the A96 stopping off everywhere between Huntly and Nairn to drop off their editions.

Other areas are covered with van runs of their own.

On the way back, we might have to pick up two or three parcels that the usual contractors can't handle quick enough, and I'll be back in Aberdeen by half-past seven.

There's not much traffic on the roads at our time. In fact, you get to know a lot of the regular cars, vans and trucks, even though you never get to speak to them.

LIBRARY

Duncan Smith

THERE'S a lot of paper in this job. We're going to be starting an electronic library shortly but, just now, we're still cutting out stories, pasting them down and filing them in packets. We file just the stories from the Press and Journal circulation area. We won't touch national ones unless they have local implications.

I couldn't tell you how many individual stories we have on file, but it must run to hundreds of thousands. Then there are all the pictures, too. Space is tight.

I've been here since 1974, but I believe when we moved up from Broad Street an awful lot of good archive material was dumped because we needed the room.

Every morning, I pick up bundles of every edition of the paper. One will go for file cuttings; one for pasting captions on to the back of pictures; one will go to be microfilmed; one will be for bound volumes of all editions, and the last will be cutting copies for journalists and reps who need to take away cuttings.

We get a lot of requests from the public for research help and we try to help as many as we can, but there are only four of us and we are a working newspaper library, not a public facility.The most common requests are from

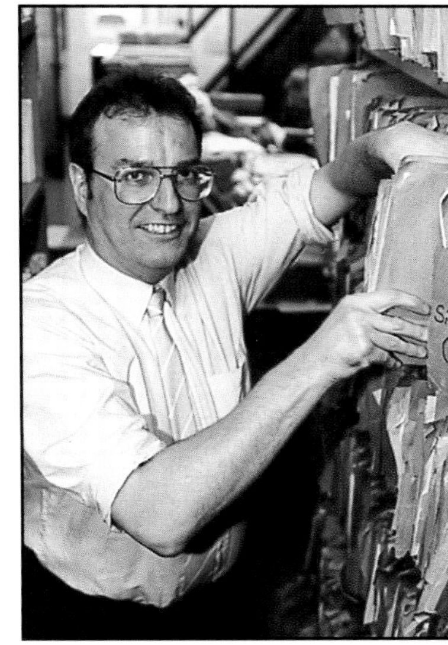

school pupils and students looking for background material, although some of them put their requests in such a way that you'd basically be doing their project for them.

We get phone calls, as well. Some of them are pretty strange. I was on New Year's Night duty a while back and the phone rang. There was a sound of a party in the background and the caller asked: 'Was it the Magnificent Seven or the Return of the Magnificent Seven that was on the TV last New Year?'

And there was the man who wanted to know what was the barometric pressure at Boddam.

MACHINE ROOM

Ricky McWilliam

BEFORE the colour press was installed in 1990, we had two old Headliner presses, and a full crew would be 28, with a working staff of 20. Now we're down to nine, with a working staff of six. This press is so hi-tech and computerised that you could black out all the windows in the control gallery and run the thing just by looking at monitors.

With the old Headliners, you could run at a maximum speed of 35,000 copies per hour. This colour press could go at 70,000, although we never do that because the P. and J. does so many editions with smallish runs that you're stopping and starting through the night.

For a 40-page P and J, we'll get through maybe 25 tonnes of paper a night — that's about 260 linear miles.

Readers used to complain about getting their hands all inky, but this press runs at such a high temperature that the ink is dry before it's off the machine.

We get paper breaks frequently, but the biggest trouble is when the paper wraps itself round a roller. You've no option but to stop the run, get into the unit and free it by hand. That could cost you between 10 minutes and half an hour. With tight deadlines,

that's time that you can't afford.

Yes, the press is complicated. I would say it was a year before I was confident with it, and I still don't know everything about it.

The person I felt sorriest for was the one who was sent in to clean the ink ducts on one of the old Headliners. He stripped off and put on a company boiler suit and climbed into the unit. It's a filthy job, anyway, but his suit ripped and the ink poured inside it and all over him.

I think he was four hours in the shower and somebody had to scrub his back for him.

After all that, he still looked inky.

MAIL ROOM

Jim Bain

I TRANSFERRED to the mail room in 1988 after 12 years in the machine room. Working with the old presses was a great job, but I could see the way the wind was blowing with new technology and the like.

So now I run the mail room. Every morning, I empty all the public letterboxes around the building; process the mat-bag mail that comes in from the district offices, and take delivery of five sacks of mail from the Post Office.

By the time I've sorted through all that, and opened whatever isn't addressed to anyone by name and worked out where to put them, and Cyril and I have delivered round the building, we're well into the morning.

The second delivery comes in and I do much the same again. Then we have mail to collect through the building and frank for going out. All Aberdeen Journals mail goes second-class, unless someone has special dispensation for a first-class item.

Even so, the company runs up £4,000 of mailing costs every 10 days, so now the Post Office has decided, as customer service, that it'll send someone to pick up our mail, instead of us having to trail down to Crown Street with it.

You see weird things in here. I remember we once ran an offer to give readers a taste of a new liquid soup in a packet. They had Lord knows how many requests for samples.

Each sample must have been worth 30p, but we paid £2.50 a time to send them out. Still, the readers were happy and that's what it's about.

But it's a great place to work. There's great camaraderie in the mail room with folk dropping in. When people ask me what qualifications I had to get a job like this I just tell them honestly: Stamina, charisma and sex appeal.

MECHANICS

Murdo Seivwright

SOMEONE worked out the other day that our 30 vans do 1,250,000 miles a year. If you added on the 137 other vehicles on the company fleet, you'd be talking a lot more than that. Considering the mileage that they cover, the breakdown and accident rate is next to nothing.

The Journals used to get Aberdeen Motors to do all its servicing, because most of the fleet was BMC and FGKs with the thripny-bit cabs, but then they started their own garage down at Pittodrie, and that was where I joined them in 1967. It was the first centrally heated garage in Aberdeen. It could be winter outside, roasting inside.

You know the stories that the P and J had a fleet of Rolls Royce vans at one time? They're all true. We had big boxes of Rolls-Royce spares still up in the loft at Pittodrie. The vans were long gone by that time. They'd done umpteen hundreds of thousands of miles and not even Rolls-Royces last for ever doing a mileage like that.

The Rolls-Royces didn't have heaters and some drivers would set a candle under the window to keep the frost off. I heard that the wipers were hand-worked.

The Garage was the first

department to move into the Lang Stracht in 1970. When we arrived, they were still assembling the presses. The reason I remember is because the engineers kept coming through and borrowing our spanners.

Nowadays, most of the fleet's diesel Transits. We did LPG-powered vans for a while and they were very successful.

In fact, when you took the LPG kit out of one van that had reached the end of its time, you could put it into the replacement and it would do another 100,000, and the same again after that.

The only reason we changed was that diesel was cheaper.

MESSENGERS

John Allan

I WAS a plasterer for 49 years until I retired, then my son, who works for the Journals, suggested I could get a part-time job at the Lang Stracht. I've been a night messenger with the Press and Journal for seven years now.

There are two of us. Fred does Sunday, Monday, Tuesday. I do Wednesday, Thursday, Friday.

When I started, it was a full-sized Wire Room and all the teleprinters were spewing out stories from all the news agencies and district offices. What an amount of paper we got through. We'd have to take the stories to the right sub-editor or reporter.

Now that everything's electronic, and the Wire Room's a quarter of the size, we don't have that to do. The stories go straight into the computers and the journalists call them up on their screens.

My day starts at teatime when I hand out copies of that day's Evening Express to the Press and Journal subs. Then I empty all the EE buckets.

Then the photographers and the specialist desks and the newsdesk start printing out the lists of stories they've been working on, so they can take them to the Editor's big conference at quarter to six. You can disappear in paper at that time.

By ten, I'm photocopying page plans for the subs. Then, at half-past eleven, the first edition's coming off the press, so I go through to Dispatch and pick up an armful for handing out to all the folk still in the building.

My last job is boxing up all the audit copies. Every story is duplicated and printed out and filed in a dated cardboard box, in case of legal problems later.

By midnight, I'm pulling on my coat. I enjoy my job. I like the company. I'd been thinking about retiring but, after my wife died, I thought it would be better to keep going.

And it gets ye oot o the hoose.

NIGHT EDITOR

Stewart Fairlie

AFTER the Editor goes home in the evening, the responsibility for the paper stops with me. I read as much as possible before it prints, but it's not possible to read every word. You have to rely on subs and newsdesk to do their jobs. I suppose this is basically a firefighting job; spotting problems before they blow up and sorting them out if they do. The more controversial items will be referred to me for a decision, but you develop a sixth sense about where less-obvious dangers might lurk.

I have to do an overnight report for the Editor, explaining where any difficulties arose, why such-and-such a page was late; why an ad didn't turn up from Advertising; why we missed an edition deadline, and so on.

The worst we've had was a page 40 minutes late, but that wasn't an Editorial problem; it got lost electronically. I can adjust deadlines, but I hardly ever do.

We get remarkably few calls from the public late at night. The newsdesk tend to screen them before they get to me. You get the odd complaint, but that's usually about something in the Evening Express.

My role is more specialist than purely Editorial in that it merges the Editorial function with Production, and that's the aspect I like most. You have to appreciate how other departments have to operate and the difficulties they have.

I finish at about three. I've worked nights for 11 years and you adjust home life to cope.

In the morning, you open rival newspapers with a sense of foreboding, especially if you've decided to treat a late-breaking story one way, and the others have gone another route completely. Or, worse, if one of them has a story we've missed. But that's the job — making the best decision you can at the time.

PAGE ASSEMBLY

Susan Bell

MY ART teacher at Glasgow High School always told me that I would never be an artist, so can you imagine the thrill I had the day I became an editorial artist at the Press and Journal? I'd proved her wrong.

Now, I'm Editorial Production Supervisor, which means I oversee a section of eight full-time and two-part time people who are responsible for assembling most of the Editorial pages each night.

Basically, we translate the page designs drawn up by the sub-editors on to the computer, and then take the text that they have edited and the pictures and illustrations that they have chosen and compile them electronically into finished pages.

In some ways, we're the last people to see them before they're printed, and it's quite something to start at the beginning of the evening with a row of blank computer screens and end up with a printed newspaper come early morning. I love this job.

It can be exceptionally busy. We'll do maybe 20 pages for the first edition, but then we'll have to redo all the pages that change for the following edition, and the edition after that, and the edition after that, until all 11 have been done. Some nights, we'll put through 20 pages for the first edition and then another 63 black-and-white pages and 12 colour by the time the full run of editions has gone.

Page Three is the busiest. It's the local-news page, so it's more or less a wholesale clearout from edition to edition.

With others, you're updating stories as developments happen, or including breaking stories, or making the pictures more relevant to that edition's area.

What really pleases me is that I'm a woman in an editorial-production job that traditionally would have been done by a man.

PAPER GIRLS

Lisa Mackie

I STARTED delivering papers when I was 13 and I've been doing it for the past three years. It was a good way to earn some extra cash because it's not every job that can fit round school time and homework.

I was a bit apprehensive the first time I turned up, but the newsagent was very good and I had someone to guide me through it for about the first week.

I get up at six-thirty and I'm usually at the paper shop by seven. The papers will have been counted for me, and I go through them just to be sure that everything's OK and to see if anyone has stopped their paper for their holidays.

Then I just go out and deliver them. There are usually about 50 papers on my round, which is a bit of a weight when you start out, but it gets better as you go on. I take about an hour to do my round, but I take an hour and a half on Saturdays because I go a bit slower.

I'm usually back at the house by eight on schooldays and then I go off to school. I'm at Kemnay Academy.

There's never really any problem with the round. Sometimes, you go on automatic pilot and deliver

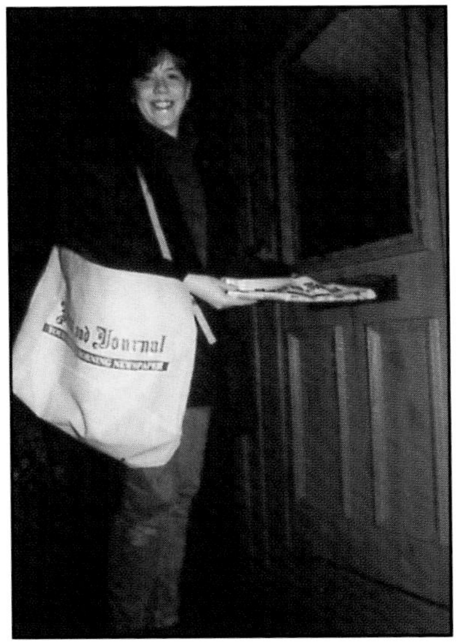

a paper to a household that's on holiday, just because you've always delivered a paper there and it's a habit, but that doesn't happen often.

When it's exam time, my family helps out. My mum wants me to be able to concentrate on the exams so she or my brother helped out with my round last time.

I don't mind the early mornings so much, and I'll probably keep doing the paper deliveries until I leave school. Then I want to go to Aberdeen University and study medicine.

And, yes, we get the Press and Journal at home.

PHOTOGRAPHERS

Sandy McCook

I WAS once asked to go down to a mountaineering-equipment shop in George Street and take a photograph of a camel. If possible, I was to take the camel down to the beach for its picture. So I went along to the shop and asked for a look at this camel, and all I got was stunned silence. It turned out that the only camel connection was a guy who was at the shop to pick up expedition gear he was getting to go on a jungle expedition sponsored by Camel cigarettes. Sometimes, the message gets garbled.

I didn't always want to be a photographer. I fancied architecture, but my father's a photographer and I'd learned the trade from him, so I went to college in Edinburgh for three years and decided that I really wanted to do Press photography.

I applied to the Press and Journal. I was interviewed by Peter Watson, who was Editor, and I was accepted.

My first job was on October 20, 1980, when I had to go to the Victoria Park in Aberdeen and do a picture of sweeping up leaves, to convey the change in the seasons.

It's the variety that I like. One minute, you'll be doing mood pictures, and the next it's hard

news. I've done work at Piper Alpha, Lockerbie, Dunblane and with the Royal Family.

I've been at bomb scares and explosions. I've done pictures out of biplanes and microlights.

One of the big changes in picture coverage is that we've stopped doing cheque presentations and the like. Machine-gun pictures, we called them, because everyone was always lined up.

People get very upset when you say No, but they'd get better coverage if they gave us some advance notice and let us cover the actual event that raised all the money. Cheque presentations are just cheap adverts for banks.

PROCESS

Alex Rae

IF YOU looked at a Press and Journal of 10 years ago, you'd be amazed by how many more pictures we're using these days. We can get through 180 different pictures a night with 11 editions.

We're the department that does the electronic scans of all the photographs — mostly slides, but some prints — for use in the paper. In the days before Apple Macintosh computers, we also took the full-sized composed pages from the old caseroom and photographed them on flatbed cameras, which gave us full-sized page negatives from which printing plates were made. We used another type of camera, to reproduce illustrations on bromide paper, which the caseroom used in paste-up.

But the caseroom and all that old technology has gone and our job has changed, as well. And we're doing colour, which is the big change that the public sees.

When we started doing colour, we were all pretty much feeling our way. We started by hand-planning, which was satisfactory, but slow. You couldn't do efficient late changes on the night for editionising or if a late story broke.

The new system is better; we can recrop pictures from edition to edition and include a lot more local pictures, exclusive to their own edition. It helps to reinforce the idea that the P&J is the daily paper for any given community.

I would say we're using more-imaginative pictures now. We're certainly using them bigger and giving them better displays.

Yes, I'm sorry to see all the old caseroom skills go, but that's the march of progress. Some of the camaraderie of the old days you'd never beat.

Now we're using skills that are just as demanding. They're different; they're more a mental challenge and less manual, but they're just as much skills.

PROMOTIONS

Susan Cook

I'D ACTUALLY wanted to get into personnel management when I was doing my course in Edinburgh, but my dad said my personality was more suited to PR.

Then I saw the advertisement for this job. I started in January, 1992, and I haven't looked back. I love my job. There's never a day that I wake up not looking forward to coming in.

I do all the promotional activity for the Press and Journal. That includes event management, hospitality, competitions, the collect-token offers and our public relations.

Sometimes, I'll be juggling 10 projects at once, which makes life busy, but it's fine by me because I like the variety and, anyway, if I get stuck with one I can put it to one side for a while and start on something else. The events are things like cookery demos, and I have a hand in the Pro-Cel-Am golf tourney that the paper runs. It really lifts you when you hear people leaving an event and saying to each other what a good time they've had. It's what the job's all about.

I try to work six or eight weeks ahead of myself. In June, I look ahead to the schools going back and work out a promotional campaign so that the summer lull in paper sales picks up. Same after Christmas.

I wouldn't say I've had any disasters, but I hadn't long started when we ran a promotion to collect tokens for a free litre of ice-cream. I forgot to put on *subject to availability*. The poor man had queues and queues and queues outside his shop and he ran out of ice-cream in hours.

We had a couple of hundred disappointed readers, but we wrote to them and the vouchers were honoured by the owner of the ice-cream shop. Luckily, he had a sense of humour.

You learn from your mistakes.

REPORTERS

Bruce Taylor

I'VE been a reporter at the Press and Journal Elgin office since 1970. I've never really had a hankering to do anything else. Some people might say that's a lack of ambition, which I'd probably accept, but all I can say is that I've enjoyed it.

A reporter needs to know people and to let them know that they can trust him. Trust is probably the greatest attribute in this job. You have to share people's joy and their tragedies. I've covered numerous road accidents and sudden deaths and trawler sinkings. I've been delighted to share in people's good news, too.

The most moving? Probably Piper Alpha. I flew over it in a Kinloss Nimrod just hours after it had happened and, I'll tell you, it just welled up in my throat. Oil can never be too dear.

I liked covering the old town councils: Burghead and Rothes, for example. I didn't drive so I had to do it all by bus. It's no fun in the middle of Burghead on a cold winter's night when the wind's blowing you off your feet.

Some reporters are always looking for the scoop and they're fed up with anything less. But I always take the attitude that the parish-pump material is just as widely read as the big stuff.

No matter how insignificant something might appear to a reporter, it'll be highly significant to someone, and that's why the Press and Journal is read from cover to cover.

I pride myself that I know my patch. There are 80,000 people in Moray and I'd hope that if something happened anywhere, there would be someone I would know who would point me in the right direction.

The hours are long, yes, but I never grudged them.

Well, I probably neglected my own family life for the sake of the Press and Journal, but I only see that now.

SECRETARIES

Morina Alexander

BEING an editorial secretary at the Inverness office was like fitting a big jigsaw together.

While the journalists got on with their stories, I would have to be in contact with all the freelance correspondents throughout the Highlands, finding out what they were offering that day, arranging pictures and being sure the whole thing came together on time.

Often I've been galloping along the platform at Inverness Station shouting at the guard: 'Don't you blow that whistle!' until I got an envelope with a picture safely on board to Aberdeen.

Many's the night I've been at home and the phone has rung and it's the office asking: 'Are you sure you put that picture on the Aberdeen train? It hasn't turned up.' And then you spent the night lying awake wondering if you had or not. But you always opened the paper the next morning and there it was.

In those days I'd be daily on the phone to freelances like Iain Grant at Thurso, Bill Lucas at Stornoway, Tony MacMillan at Fort William and Jimmy Henderson at Golspie, and we'd have a blether and they'd tell me what was on their news schedule.

Now it's all electronic and it goes down the computer line from us

to Aberdeen so it cuts down the human contact.

How do Highlanders look on the Press and Journal? I would say as their daily paper, because any story anywhere in the North is well covered by the P and J. I know that by the number of calls I get from organisations, asking if they can have cuttings because we've given the whole story.

I've been very lucky. I've had all the buzz of news-gathering with none of the hassle of producing the stories. And I've been lucky with my job and my colleagues.

You read about people suffering from stress at work and you can't help feeling sorry for them.

SECURITY

Gordon Forbes

THE Journals building sits on a short cut from Summerhill to Mastrick and we used to have folk wandering back and forth on the premises. They had nothing to do with the Journals, and we couldn't have told you who they were or what they were doing walking along outside the building. It was just a nightmare.

So a few years ago the company beefed up the security. Well, you could have had anybody wandering through the building lifting stuff.

All the staff were issued with passes and we built a gatehouse at the main entrance and covered the other two with video systems. Some of the staff don't like showing their passes. The ones who have been here for twenty or twenty-five years think they shouldn't have to, but the managing director shows his pass every morning — 'Good morning, Mr Scott' — so if it's good enough for him . . .

The public don't seem to mind the security measures, although you get some visitors who'll say; 'But I've never needed a pass before and I've been visiting the Journals for years', and we'll say: 'Well, ye need a pass noo.'

Some we'll tell to park in the visitors' car park and when they

find out that they'll have to walk to the front door, they just turn about and leave. If they can't get their car to the door, they don't want to know.

But that's just security. You couldn't do it any other way.

It's a long shift. We do 12 hours at a time, with patrols every twenty minutes and you're knackered at the end of it. I've been here for three years.

Problems? Not really. The staff here are a friendly bunch and you get on first-name terms very quickly. The only thing is that we're stuck out here in the gatehouse. We don't get to speak to people the same.

SUB-EDITORS

Lindsay Macdonald

PEOPLE open their paper over breakfast and see 34 pages or whatever, but they don't realise that that's only about a third of the total output. By the time you account for all 11 editions, up to 100 different P and J pages will have been subbed, laid out and printed every morning.

Sub-editors are the dozen or so bodies on any one night who take all the raw copy and pictures from staff, agencies and correspondents and decide how (or if) it will appear in the paper.

The most satisfying part of my subbing job is being in charge of a page, be it World News, Business or General (UK) News, and making the decisions on what gets binned, what gets cut, what needs more, which gets prominence and then seeing the result printed.

Many readers don't realise we can use only a fraction of the stuff we receive on these pages for space reasons.

You make the decisions by trying to envisage the interests and tastes of the reader. This is a gamble because you're in danger of having the wrong idea entirely and assuming that they're preoccupied with flower-show results or not at all interested in the war in Chechnya, or vice

versa. You try to have an interesting mix.

Subs used to do a lot of rewriting because freelance copy would land raw on our desks, but now the newsdesk sorts wheat from chaff. It makes our job easier.

I know readers point at spelling mistakes and shake their heads. If it's consolation, we're more annoyed by mistakes than anyone, but you must understand the continuous pressure and deadlines of turning out 11 newspapers a night.

By the time we get a minute to sit and read a newly printed paper, it's often past 3am and, sadly, too late to do anything about it.

SWITCHBOARD
May Singer

WHEN I joined the company in 1975, we had two huge switchboards. I suppose they were modern for their day, but compared to the equipment now, they would look ancient.

Now we've got a voice-connect system on the switchboard, we're not the first point of contact for a lot of callers. The ones who know which extension they want listen to the recorded message and go straight through. We handle the callers who need help or who don't know who they need to talk to. We have 36 lines and 250 extensions to memorise, so it can get quite busy still.

We get a lot of calls which, strictly speaking, aren't P&J-related. We've had people phoning up asking: 'What's that funny smell in Union Street?' or: 'I canna get through to Pittodrie, how much are the tickets on Saturday?' You put them through to the people you think will be able to help.

You get angry callers, especially when they disagree with a story. They just have a different point of view and they're worked up, but being reasonable takes the aggression out of it.

We get compliments, too. I try to put them through to the people involved, because I think

complaints need to be balanced by compliments. Quite a few of the people offering compliments are a bit shy of speaking, though, so we can't always do it.

We have our regulars. There's one woman who phones up insisting that the buses owe her £100,000, and she wants to know what we're doing about it. She's been phoning with the same call for years. People do think that once the P&J's on the case, they're home and dry.

The voice system doesn't please everybody. We often answer a call and there'll be a silence, then this little voice will say: 'Hullo? Hullo? Are you real?'

VENDORS
Jocky Shirreffs

I STARTED vending in the Thirties. My first big story was the Jeannie Donald murder, and I'd nae lang left the school. Then there was the Germans bombing Poland. I shifted a thousand papers that day.

Now I'm seventy-seven and I'm still selling papers. I love the papers. I like meeting all the readers and I like coming into the Mastrick office to see the boys.

Woodend Hospital was my territory for thirty years. I would go round the wards selling papers, cracking jokes and talking to patients. You meet all kinds in hospital, from chief constables to entertainers to just ordinary fowk.

I ran a concert party at the hospital for a while. Well, it's important to keep fowk cheery, isn't it? Crack a few jokes. Give them a laugh. Take their mind off hospital. Then my wife died and, ach, I stopped for a while. But you get to miss the company in this job, so I went back.

I once appeared in the papers, as well as selling them. Bunty Fisher wrote a story about me many years ago and I've still got the cutting somewhere. I kept it.

For the last few years, I've been vending at the Highland Games

and the agricultural shows. I'm the man who sells the papers at the Braemar Gathering, the Lonach, Aboyne Games, Keith Show, Turriff Show and plenty others. Robbie Shepherd's a good pal. I ken a'body and a'body kens me.

I've thought about retiring, but to be honest with you, I like the job too much, so I'll maybe go out round all the shows again next summer if I can. I haven't made up my mind yet.

Anyway, I'm happiest doing the shows. I wouldn't like to be standing at the top of Market Street these days. Nae at my age. The weather wid kill ye.

TALL SHIPS
Press and Journal
Barbour
What's On
Offshore Journal
Lifestyle
Research revises human BSE risk upwards
Man in 200ft death plunge
Thanks a million for lifesaving scanner
False alarm
Charged
Hearts
final

CHAPTER X

The Next 250

TODAY, the Press and Journal can boast a record unequalled in British and world newspapers. It remains Britain's oldest daily paper by a large margin. It is the third-oldest English-language paper in the world. It is Britain's biggest-selling regional morning. Its penetration throughout its circulation area is among the highest in the EU. In Grampian, the Highlands and Islands, every other household contains a Press and Journal at some point in the week. In parts of agricultural Aberdeenshire, that rises to nine out of ten households every day of every week.

The core of this potent recipe can be traced back to founder James Chalmers, post-Culloden. He judged that the most successful newspaper would be the one that best reflected its readers and their concerns; the paper which inveigled itself so deeply into the fabric of its community that it became part of it.

Two hundred and fifty years later, when the activities of many newspapers have ensured that their readers have become cynical and mistrusting, the Press and Journal strives to live up to the Chalmers founding tenet, even although that has become immeasurably more difficult and challenging since Issue One fluttered on to the streets.

Many readers identify intensely with the Press and Journal. 'They're not wishy-washy in their views,' said Aberdeen Journals managing director Alan Scott. 'In 1988, we invited the team who had designed the Independent to redesign the Press and Journal. Not long after the new-look paper hit the streets, I was approached by one reader who demanded: "What the devil do you think you're doing to my paper?"

'*My* paper. He was being critical, but he'd paid us the biggest compliment we could have had. I was delighted.'

Now the Press and Journal is casting its net wider. It was founded purely for Aberdeen. By the end of the 1700s, it had spread through the rural

LEFT
Managing director Alan Scott took over the hot seat at Aberdeen Journals Ltd. in 1984.

RIGHT
Newsagents — the last vital link in getting papers delivered efficiently every morning.

North-east and Moray to Inverness. Over the next century, it pushed up the East Coast to Wick and down to Montrose. By 1960, it was covering all of the Highlands, Islands and Grampian. Now, it covers virtually everywhere north of the Central Belt.

From four district offices after World War II — in Inverness, Elgin, Buchan and Banff — the paper now has staff operating from nine — Dingwall, Fort William, Inverness, Elgin, Banff, Peterhead, Stonehaven and Forfar. Stirling was added in 1994 and its commercial, circulation and editorial results have broken all expectations, ahead of plan.

From Jimmy Grant's seven daily editions in 1965, the paper now turns out 11, six days a week, making the Press and Journal the world's most editionised newspaper. Mastrick HQ attracts delegations from newspaper publishers throughout the world, curious to learn how such a complex edition structure is controlled nightly, and how such a big and diverse circulation area is covered from just one printing centre with so few problems. 'We're serving 20% of the land

ABOVE
The van network of Aberdeen Journals is the most extensive of any newspaper publisher in Britain.

RIGHT
Chief sub-editor Jimmy Urquhart (seated) and assistant chief sub Jay Ferrier discuss use of pictures.

FIRE
ALARM

mass of the UK,' said Allister Shacklock, of the circulation department. 'That's bigger than the whole of Switzerland, and that makes circulation one of the trickier aspects of producing the paper.

'We use anything and everything to get the papers to readers as soon as possible. We've our vans, of course, but we also use post, milkmen, buses, trains, planes and taxis. On one occasion, when the road to Buchan was blocked, we chartered a trawler.'

Aberdeen Journals has also invested heavily in technology. At the end of 1990, a £10million full-colour press came on-line,

LEFT
Vendors, familiar faces on city streets.

ABOVE
All forms of distribution are pressed into service to try to cover the vast circulation area as efficiently and quickly as possible, from British Airways to the friendly milkie.

FAR RIGHT
The Goss Colorliner press is capable of 75,000 copies an hour.

and is now so much part of the Press and Journal and Evening Express that pre-1990 black-and-white papers seem so dated.

The new press can print 75,000 copies an hour, or 21 copies a second — a distinct advance on James Chalmers and his single-sheet hand press, turning out 240 copies an hour.

The company is also looking ahead at electronic publishing and, in May, 1997, launched its own site on the World Wide Web. 'There is no doubt that the electronic-publishing revolution will gain pace and it is vital that newspapers are in a position to move with the times,' said current Editor Derek Tucker.

'The day when ink on paper is rendered obsolete will not happen in my lifetime, but it is clear that there is a significant number of people who, for various reasons, would prefer to receive their Press and Journal electronically.

'The trick will be in keeping pace with changes in reader expectations.

'No one is making significant money out of supplying information on the Internet at present, but someone, somewhere, will do so some time. We'll be there with them.'

For the moment, the Press and Journal is consolidating in its new, broader market, and that

ABOVE
Advertising Manager Janis Gallon Smith chairs a meeting of her senior executives.

LEFT
Putting a face to the voices at the end of the phone. The Tele-Ads operators advise on how best to promote items for sale in Classified columns.

applies to advertising, as much as circulation and editorial.

'If you stand still in this game, you're dead,' said advertising manager Janis Smith. 'The competition is just so intense. There's this laughable myth that the Press and Journal has a monopoly on advertising in northern Scotland and that we have it easy. Don't you believe it. We have some of the strongest weekly papers in the country here. We have commercial radio. We have national papers who have realised suddenly that Scotland exists. We have commercial TV. It's incredibly tough.

'But people keep coming back to the Press and Journal because they find that it works best for them. An advertisement is not expensive if it sells the product, and 99% of our advertisers are successful. If you want to know how well the economy of any area of Britain is doing look at the number of pages of classified ads in the regional daily. It's an extraordinarily accurate gauge.'

'It's certainly a danger that any newspaper company becomes too obsessed with the area just a few miles round its production centre,' said Alan Scott. 'When I arrived in 1984, there was a sign of that creeping into this company. We were too Aberdeen-centred commercially and editorially. The Highlands are quite distinct from Aberdeen and the North-east and we needed to recognise that. It was important that Inverness and the North had autonomy from our Aberdeen people. I also thought we were a little too reliant on oil-based revenue, and the market dip in 1986 proved the point. We're more diverse now.

'Yes, we've gone through great upheaval. The whole industry has, and we're no different. But no one at Aberdeen Journals was sacked because of new technology.

'Some accepted voluntary-severance packages, and others were retrained in other parts of the operation. No other newspaper company can say the same, and I'm proud of that.'

There comes a time in every working day when you have to catch up with the news.

we can't afford
No gun ban

ABOVE
Every evening at 5.45pm the Editor, Derek Tucker (seated, left) calls a meeting in his office to hear what his various departments are offering for use in next day's paper. This is the meeting which outlines the shape of all 11 editions and forms the paper's opinion on an issue of the day.

LEFT
Busy newsdesk controls the flow of stories.

THE Press and Journal broke new ground in 1992. After 245 years and 21 Scots as Editors, the company appointed its first Sassenach to the hot seat. The 22nd Editor, Derek Tucker, arrived from the English West Midlands to meet a somewhat wary workforce.

'One of the first things I did was go on a private tour of the circulation area,' he said. 'I needed to see it first-hand. You can't run a paper properly until you've seen all its circulation area and met the people and listened to them.

'Later, we chartered a mobile exhibition centre and stopped in every major town from the North Coast to Tayside and invited people to come and meet us. We weren't sure if people would want to come to see a static exhibition about the Press and Journal, but we were amazed by the response. People showed great interest and offered positive feedback. The thing that kept coming across was that this was their paper, their paper, their paper, and they didn't want me to tamper with it.'

At Peterhead, the exhibition centre dropped anchor in the middle of town and placards invited townsfolk to step inside to meet the Editor. Two elderly ladies climbed inside warily to survey the surroundings. Eventually, and extremely reluctantly, they approached Derek Tucker to ask where the Press and Journal Editor was.

'You're speaking to him,' he said. 'I'm the Press and Journal Editor.'

They looked at each other, mildly alarmed, then looked back at him. 'If ye dinna mind me sayin,' said one, 'it's a damned

disgrace that the P and J Editor's English.'

'Funnily enough,' he said later, 'I've never minded the English.'

Derek Tucker says his changes have been evolutionary, not revolutionary. 'I've tried to sharpen up the news content and broaden the outlook, but I'm keen to follow the Jimmy Grant philosophy of having communities feel that the Press and Journal is *their* paper and knows *their* area. If a new minister takes over in a village, we should be the means by which that news is spread. The same goes for a new beat bobby, or doctor or head teacher. Now that we have introduced the training scheme, we'll be able to do that much better.'

LEFT
Still the United Kingdom's only full-time staff fisheries journalist, Fishing Editor Bob Kennedy.

ABOVE
Matters agricultural, meanwhile, are the field of Farming Editor Joe Watson.

RIGHT
And coverage of the Dons is the business of football writer Michael Grant.

In 1996, Aberdeen Journals founded an in-house journalism course, specifically for aspiring journalists from within the circulation area.

Over a year of aptitude tests, hundreds of applicants were whittled down to the nine best, who then began an intensive programme covering news values, use of English, newspaper ethics, interview skills, politics, law, local government, shorthand and the many other skills which professional journalists must deploy every day — none more than a genuine interest in people.

'We wanted to give something back to the area,' said the Editor, 'and we felt that the specific needs of the Press and Journal and our readers meant that we couldn't just rely on importing journalists from anywhere in the country, who would use us and our readers as a handy paragraph on their CVs, then leave after 18 months. You need sound local knowledge on a regional paper. The best way to acquire that is to pick plum people from the area itself and train them to your standards.

'I think one of the greatest mistakes in journalism recruitment is to insist on graduates only. Trainees need to be interested in other people, not themselves. That's why our first intake of journalism students is made up entirely of school-leavers. They are all people who could have sailed into university, but they are burning to do this job, and we're doing everything we can to help them.

'Apart from that, we have kept all the Press and Journal strengths. We still print later than any other daily paper circulating in the northern half of Scotland, so we're frequently breaking news and sports stories that the others still can't.

'We're still not aligned to any political party, although every politician who can wield a ruler thinks his party gets a rough deal from us. They are all equally annoyed at some time or another, and that's the way I want to keep it.'

AT THE beginning of 1996, the Thomson Organisation sold Aberdeen Journals to another newspaper group. Northcliffe, the regional-papers stablemate of the Daily Mail, bought the company after close bidding. There was historical justice in the sale, as anyone familiar with the company history knew. In 1928, Northcliffe was the company that stumbled at the last hurdle to buy the Aberdeen papers, outmanoeuvred by the Berry brothers and the company's own management. To be patient for 68 years is remarkable in any industry. In newspapers, it is unheard of.

'I still have total admiration for the Press and Journal,' said Harry Roulston, Editor from 1986 to 1992. 'We promoted it as the complete morning newspaper, and that's exactly what it still is. It's a simple concept, but exceptionally difficult to put into place, and even more difficult to keep doing day after day after day for so many editions.'

'People always imagine that the Press and Journal is parochial,' said Peter Watson, Editor from 1975 to 1986. 'If, by that, they mean it takes a close interest in what is going on in the smallest corners of the circulation area, then I'm delighted. If they think that the paper is obsessed with minutiae to the exclusion of world events, then, I'm sorry, but they haven't looked at the Press and Journal. It has an extraordinarily broad, international outlook, for a paper that achieves so much within its area.'

All the surviving Editors — Ken

ABOVE
Heartland of Press and Journal sales, the wee country shop and post office which is as much focal point of the community as public service.

Peters, Peter Watson, Harry Roulston and incumbent Derek Tucker — are proud of the extraordinary number of good causes the Press and Journal has supported, or the public campaigns it has led. Among them are the fund-raising campaign for the1876 Dee ferry disaster, which killed 32; the Boer War widows' fund; numerous campaigns for the families of men killed in fishing boats; the Willing Shilling fund to provide holidays for children from poor city families; the World War II comforts fund; scholarships to Aberdeen University; Pearl Murray's guide-dogs campaigns of the 1960s, and a score of public-interest campaigns from water safety to road safety, from hospital equipment to school equipment.

Indeed, readers have come to expect that the Press and Journal will back campaigns in the public interest, and plaques throughout the North of Scotland referring to the Press and Journal and its readers show they are disappointed very rarely.

'I wonder what James Chalmers would make of his brainchild now,' said Derek Tucker. 'I wonder if he realised it would survive for so long and would work itself so deeply into the fabric of the whole of the North of Scotland.

'What other publication knows its area's heritage and culture and people so well, and has known them for two and a half centuries?

'Which other paper has such a long memory? Or tries so scrupulously to be fair to all sides? Or takes an Editorial line based not on politics or self-interest or the bottom line of the newspaper company itself, but on purely one criterion: what will do the most good for the most people in the area?

'Long may that remain true of the Press and Journal. I raise my glass to her.

'Here's to the next two hundred and fifty.'

Editorship stretching back more than 40 years. From left: Ken Peters (1956-1960) was subsequently the longest-serving managing director of Aberdeen Journals this century; Peter Watson (1975-1987) guided the paper through some of its greatest technological change; current Editor Derek Tucker (1992-), the first Englishman in the hot seat, has broadened the paper's national outlook, and Harry Roulston (1987-1992) piloted his paper through great industrial upheaval and held the paper's circulation steady while regionals throughout Britain went into decline.

Press and Journal

Afterword

LIKE most people of my vintage who were born and raised in the northern half of Scotland, I grew up with the Press and Journal. The paper was an integral part of our household for far longer than I can remember. It is certainly impossible for me to recall a time when "the daily", as it was known throughout the howe and beyond, was not readily to hand.

From the moment it dropped through the letterbox at 7.45am until the moment the last light was turned off, the P and J was a constant companion, guide, informant and authority; not the 25-minute flick-through that market analysts will tell you is the lot of any modern morning paper (it was too expensive for that, and this was 1960s Aberdeenshire), but a publication which served its many purposes repeatedly throughout each day.

The daily kept us abreast of what was happening nationally, regionally and locally, but it did much more. It helped form opinions. It sparked tea-table discussions and, on several heated occasions, settled arguments, such was our trust. Besides, no serious student of Births, Deaths and Marriages could have contemplated life without the Press and Journal.

Even by the following morning, when the paper had yielded its all and lay exhausted at the end of the settee, it had not quite outlived its usefulness. With innate understanding of the transience of journalism, my mother would flick it out into five or six separate sheets and set the fire with it. I remain convinced that the image of mothers lighting fires with hard-wrought words gives many Scottish journalists their senses of proportion. It is difficult to preen when you know that your deftly turned phrases will bear kindling (or wrap fish, or floor kennels) within 48 hours. Few other professions have such constant and healthy reminders of their relative importance.

I little thought that the Press and Journal would be the bedrock of my career, or that many of the people whose work I had read as a boy would become my colleagues. Even after induction into the trade, the Press and Journal was a means to an end; like almost all new journalists, I had promised myself that after training and completing indentures, I would be off to Fleet Street. "Within three years" was the target I had set myself but, somewhere along the way, the North-east and the Press and Journal tightened their grip and did it so gently and so subtly that I did not notice. Now, I have missed my deadline by 18 years.

When the current Editor asked me to consider writing the story of the Press and Journal, I needed no second bidding. What writer would? To be given free rein through 250 years of archives and almost all the history that has shaped modern Scotland is the journalistic equivalent of small boy and sweetie shop.

But that same challenge has brought problems. Distilling 250 years of history and the lives of thousands of newspaper people

LEFT:

Norman Harper and companion at home in the heart of the Howe of Alford.

Liverpool 35
Livingstone, Alexander 25
Lockerbie **140,**154,159
Lodge Walk 46
Logan, Jimmy 70
Lonach 163
Lonely hearts 20
Lonely Tom 113
Longhope 97,**105,118**
Lucas, Bill 161
Luftwaffe 49
Lumphanan 181

Mc

McCook, Sandy **159**
Macdonald, Alistair 97
Macdonald, Lindsay **162**
MacDonald, W.R.O. 97,134
Macduff 115
McHardy, Bruce 97
Mackie, Lisa **159**
Mackie, Maureen **153**
McLeod, James D.G. 109
MacMillan, Tony 161
MacQueen, Dr Ian 85-87
MacRae, Duncan 61,83,84,90,96,97,**102,137,**147
MacSporran, Hector 88,**89**
McWilliam, Ricky **156**

M

Marischal College 10, 12, 24
Market Street, Aberdeen 163
Marnoch 113
Mastrick 125,133,134,162,163,166
Maxwell, William 32,33,35,38,39,41,186
Mearns 96
Meigle 181
Menzies, James **89**,96
Menzies, John 155
Meston, Sandy 84,90,97
Millar, Jimmy 110
Miller, Willie 182
Mitchell, James Leslie 34-35
Mitchell & Muil 153
Montgomery, Lynn **141**
Montrose 166
Moonie, Val 88,97
Moray 161,166
Moray and Nairn Gazette 78
Munro, Alex 97,131,132
Murray, Pearl 62,85,96,134,176
Murray, William 21-23
Music Hall 58

N

Nairn 155,182
National Union of Journalists (NUJ) 144-148
Ness, George 85
News of the World 154
Nicol, James 10,12
North Anderson Driver 129
North Briton 26
North Star, Dingwall 83
North of Scotland Gazette 27
North of Scotland Newspaper Printing Company 27
Northcliffe Newspapers Ltd. 43,175
Northern Gazette 34

O

Ogilvies 120
Oil discovered **125,**136
Old Deer 13
Oldmeldrum 15,19
Olympic Games 29
Operation Mastrick 125-129
Orkney 183
Oslo 147
Outrams 70
Owens, Jesse 46

P

Palace Hotel, Aberdeen **51**
Pennan 59,**60**,103
Perth 117,140,183
Perth Advertiser 26
Peterhead 15,**52**,103,136,152,166,173
Peters, Kenneth J. 61,63,75,77,78,80,81,87,90,93,117, 120,123,125,**128,**129,176,**177**
Piper Alpha explosion **139**,141,154,159,161
Pittodrie 157,163
Playhouse Cinema, Aberdeen 83
Ponjavi, Maria 133,134
Portknockie 109
Portsoy 113
Pratt Report into AJL 74
Press and Journal 49,52,55,57,59,61,62,63,64,71,73,74, 75,77,78,80,83,84,86,88,89,93,94,96, 97,99,101,103,104,105,106,109,115, 119,126,135,136,140,141,148,151, 152,155,156,157,159,160,161,162, 165,169,171,173,175,176,179,185, 186
Pressly, David 31
Prieg, Günther 133,134
Priestly, Helen 46,48
Profumo, John 70
Proof-readers **69**
Prospect Terrace 53

Q

Queen Elizabeth II **64,87**,88,89
Queen Mother **5,68**,69,**135**
Queen Street 123,125
Queen Victoria 29

R

R101 crash 46

Rae, Alex **160**
Rangers FC 180
Robertson, Harry 86,92
Rolls-Royce 157
Ross-shire 84
Rothes 161
Roulston, Harry
141,144,148,175,176,**177**
Royal Artillery 80

S

Savoy Hotel 71
Scots Champion 27
Scotsman
26,42,69,145
Scott, Alan
137,144,145,146,147,148,162,**164**,
165,171
Scott of the Antarctic 29
Scottish Co-operative Movement
70,**72**
Scottish Labour Party 69
Scott Lithgow 181
Scottish Television 70,71
Seivwright, Murdo **157**
Shacklock, Allister
152,166
Shepherd, Robbie
163,181
Shetland
136,140
Shirreffs, Jocky **163**
Shore Porters Society 23
Simpson, Ethel
51,52,53,58,84,88,**89**,90,96,131,135,
136
Simpson, Norman 86
Singer, May **163**
Skye 181
Smith, Donovan
97,133
Smith, Duncan **155**
Smith, George Ley
55,**58**-59,61,80,83
Smith, James 25
Smith, Janis Gallon
170,171
Smith, Lorraine **151**
St Valéry en Caux 55
Station Hotel, Aberdeen 89
Statue of Liberty 29
Steam press 36
Stevenson, Eric
88,141
Stirling 166
Strachan, Ted
80,136
Strichen 62
Stonehaven
56,117,166,181
Stornoway 161
Strath, Chief Constable 113
Stromness 181
STUC 29
Subbing
33,35,**51**,179
Suffragettes 29
Summerhill 162
Sunday Times 71,96
Sutherland 84
Sutherland, David 97
Sutherland, Jackie 92

T

Tarland 181
Tarves 13
Tavendale, Iain **153**
Tay Bridge 29
Taylor, Bruce **161**
Tevendale, Brian 88-89
Thatcher, Margaret **141**
Thomson, Roy (later Lord)
64,67,68,69,**70**,**73**,74,77,78,80,
83,117,**128**,129,136
Thomson Regional Newspapers
75,137,145,175
Thomson, Steve **154**
Thurso
113,161
Titanic
29,**178**
Tivoli Theatre 34
Tomintoul 180
Torphins 182
Torry, Aberdeen **50**
Tough, Peter 42
Trams
31,**109**
Tucker, Derek
169,**173**,176,**177**
Turriff
62,**115**
Turriff Show
131,163
Typhoid epidemic of 1964
84-86,85-88
Tyrebagger 15

U

Udny **176**
Union Street,Aberdeen
28,35,38,41,**44**,51,87,117,120,163
Upperkirkgate 120
Urquhart, Jimmy
141,**167**
Urquhart Road murder 46-48

V

Veitch, Wm.
32,42,51,55,61,62,**67**,**121**,186

W

Walker, Brian **155**
Waterloo page **22**
Watson, Joe **174**
Watson, Peter
96,97,134,136,159,175,176,**177**
Watt, Hamish 113
Weekly Journal
42,52,**61**,71
Westburn Road 129
Wester Ross 136
Whitehills 106
Wick
117,166,182
Williamson, James 87
Willing Shilling Fund 176
Wilson, George 106
Wire room
46,**59**,79
Woodend General Hospital
35,163
World War I
32,33,37
World War II
48-55,63,166,176
Wright Brothers 29

Y

Yarrow, Sir Harold 70
Younger, George 181

This book would not have been possible without the ready assistance of Bob Carter, Harry Conroy, Johnnie Duncan, George Durward, Gordon Forbes, Bill Forsyth, Tom Forsyth, George Fraser, Elaine King, Hilda Grant, Bill Jamieson, Jim Kinnaird, Ron Knox, Jimmy Lees, Duncan MacRae, Pearl Murray, Ken Peters, Alison Reid, Harry Roulston, Alan Scott, Allister Shacklock, Ethel Simpson, Janis Smith, Derek Tucker and Peter Watson.

The artworks on Pages 2, 6 and 7 are by Press and Journal editorial artist Jayne Anderson.

The non-archive photographs are by staff photographers
Steve Bain
Bob Bruce
Ian Dawson
John Lindsay
Sandy McCook
David Murray
Les Parker
Colin Rennie
and Ian Young

With thanks to Press and Journal librarian Duncan Smith and his staff
Ken Mackay
Bob Moodie
and Bob Stewart
and to the Local Studies Department of the Central Library, Aberdeen.

The archive newspapers from pages 31 to 41, and the illustrations on pages 8, 14, 33 and 36 are reproduced courtesy of Aberdeen City Council Arts and Recreation Department.